MW01491724

"This workbook is a rare gift to parents. Dr. Robinson and Ms. Gerstenzang offer a wealth of specific, practical strategies that parents (and kids) can use, every day, to help children develop improved emotional awareness, frustration tolerance, and self-control. But this is much more than a book of techniques to help soothe children in moments of emotional distress. It is also a book about how parents can strengthen their relationship with their children in ways that build lasting capacities for emotional growth and resilience. All parents, of children at all ages, will benefit from this excellent workbook."

—Kenneth Barish, PhD, Clinical Professor of Psychology, Weill Cornell Medicine; Author, *Pride and Joy: A Guide to Understanding Your Child's Emotions and Solving Family Problems*

"In this age of 'busy,' this workbook is a good reminder that parenting requires time. I think everyone who reads it will be reminded of the importance of good emotional health as a contributor to a successful and happy life. [...] The parenting suggestions are relevant and effective. The content pages are packed with all of the topics that comprise helping children learn to be emotionally healthy. [...] I really see parents liking this workbook."

—Arleta James, LPCC, Founder, Adoption and Attachment Therapy Partners, LLC

"I love the real-life examples and easy-to-understand explanations of concepts that I've seen other books make way too abstract for the average parent. This workbook empowers parents with a step-by-step roadmap to connected parent-child regulation. This is the workbook I wish I'd had both as a new parent and when I opened my parenting-focused therapy practice!"

—Nanika Coor, PsyD, Founder, Brooklyn Parent Therapy

"This is a brilliant and beautiful book, written to guide parents and their 5- to 8-year-old children through the complexities of managing their feelings, little and big, easy and hard. Robinson translates decades of developmental and scientific knowledge into accessible, lively prose, and brings humor, warmth, and compassion to the struggles we all face day to day. This gem is an incredible resource for anyone who cares about children and wants to help nurture their amazing capacities. I just loved it...it will be my 'go-to' book for parents from now on!"

—Arietta Slade, PhD, Yale Child Study Center

"If you have been feeling challenged as a parent, worrying that your child needs help learning to manage emotions, or you're a therapist seeking a book to aid families in this age group, this is the book for you! [...] One of the strengths of this book is the many examples of specific language and strategies parents can use to calm themselves down [... in situations] of big emotional displays that may cause parents to feel embarrassed, overwhelmed, or worried. In my 15+ years' work as a child and family psychologist, I have found parents often ask for and benefit from specific language of how to manage these dysregulated moments. This book has these types of examples in spades!"

—Miguelina German, PhD, Associate Clinical Professor, Department of Pediatrics & Department of Psychiatry and Behavioral Sciences, Albert Einstein College of Medicine

"The authors provide us with a master class on parenting 5- to 8-year-old children or any children with this level of emotional maturity. The workbook clearly explains often talked about parenting concepts of attunement, co-regulation, and self-regulation. But how exactly do we increase our attunement? How do we help our children calm down when they are having big feelings? This workbook provides easy-to-follow, tangible ways of putting these concepts into action. All along the authors remind us that parental self-compassion is imperative when things don't go quite as planned."

—Carolyn B. Sorkin, PhD, Founder, Sorkin Psychological Services; Director, the Child & Adolescent Externship, William Alanson White Institute

THE
Self-Regulation
WORKBOOK
for Children Ages 5 to 8

A Parent-Child Resource for Engaging in Healthy Coping Skills and Building Connection

KAHLILA ROBINSON, PhD,
in collaboration with Sarah Gerstenzang, LCSW

ULYSSES BOOKS
FOR YOUNG READERS

Published by:
Ulysses Books for Young Readers,
an imprint of Ulysses Press
32 Court Street, Suite #2109
Brooklyn, NY 11201
www.ulyssespress.com

ISBN: 978-1-64604-760-4

Printed in the United States
10 9 8 7 6 5 4 3 2 1

Acquisitions editor: Claire Sielaff
Managing editor: Claire Chun
Editor: Renee Rutledge
Proofreader: Barbara Schultz
Front cover design: Rebecca Lown
Interior design and production: Winnie Liu
Artwork from shutterstock: cover © Virinaflora; interior pages 3, 4, 7, 8, 11, 26, 29, 36, 57, 82, 89, 101, 128, 137 © GoodStudio; page 9 © Viktoria Kazakova; page 31 © woocat; page 34 © Bilbo Baggins; page 36 © Siwa Jittar; page 37 © Paranyu; page 44 © Golden Sikorka page 48 © Peter Hermes Furian; page 52 © Designsells; page 88 © lemono; page 102 © Quang Vinh Tran; page 103 © Giuseppe_R; page 103 © Julia Galuzinskaya; page 112 © Virinaflora; page 126 shells © irarusaya, pepper © WinWin artlab; page 136 © vivat

CONTENTS

INTRODUCTION

Good parenting can often feel like walking a tightrope: it requires you to stay steady and calm, maintain a delicate balance, and use your senses to predict and adjust. You need to stay in the present while having an eye toward the future. Under certain conditions, you may fall right off. Other times, you can *really* enjoy it; you remain steady, getting yourself to solid ground. This workbook covers the skills of making you a proper tightrope walker, including the art of getting back up after you fall.

We are experienced child therapists who are parents ourselves. This workbook presents the parenting concepts and strategies that have been most helpful in our own families and to the hundreds of families, parents, and children we have worked with throughout the years. We created this workbook in order to share the insights, concepts, helpful guidance, and tools we have gathered with a wider audience. As you will read, many families, including our own, face similar challenges when children are between the ages of five and eight.

Children and adults, though developmentally distinct, share many things in common as human beings. Part of what we share is that our experience of emotion can sometimes feel out of our control. This is a unique challenge for us parents and caregivers: How do we remain steady supports for our children, when our own emotions can feel overwhelming? Parenting is not like breathing, which we are born able to do. Although it is somewhat instinctive (think about how horrible it is to hear an infant cry—we just want to pick up that baby so they will stop!), a lot of us are learning on the job. Parenting at our best includes offering ourselves grace and self-compassion when we don't get things quite right.

Children are often doing the best they can, as well. Kids do not like to feel out of control of their emotions. In fact, when kids lose control it is because they are still learning the complex skill of emotion regulation, not because they are trying to drive us crazy.

The parents we work with in our therapy practices benefit from being consistent, fair, and firm with their children. They offer lots of warmth and opportunities to bond. They establish reasonable limits and follow through. They have insight on their own attachment history and the ways that influences their parenting. They model their ability to reflect on their own feelings, repair ruptures, do their best to stay well-regulated, and help their child explore their feelings. When you focus on developing these skills, your child will benefit.

The five- to eight-year old children we are talking about in this book are truly unique. At this age their personalities are flourishing! They have started to understand, be sensitive to, and curious about emotions in themselves and others. They are highly imaginative, funny, and even wise! They can ask existential questions, and pause to notice things that adults take for granted. The other day I overhead an eight-year-old ask her parent, "Why do people die?" As I started thinking of how one might answer such a deep question, I heard her answer it for herself: "So that the world doesn't become too crowded! If no one died, there would be no space for the people who are being born." Phew! I shook my head in amazement at the question, and the answer.

Kids this age can be remarkably observant and insightful. Many are willing to explore their emotions and to learn new skills to help them feel better and get along well with their family. Although there will always be some challenges that are too hard for kids to figure out, at this age it is still appropriate to ask children to use their minds to identify the source of their internal problems (Novick and Novick 2010). Despite all of their amazing growth and abilities, five- to eight-year-olds continue to need help from adults in dealing with "big" emotions.

For parents who are doing their best to take care of their children, we hope using this workbook can offer peace of mind in navigating the good, the bad, and the crazy-making of parenting kids this age. Included are parenting strategies meant to support both parent and child self-regulation and those that offer insight into what kids can and cannot do emotionally. For children, this workbook offers an interactive approach to reflect on feelings and practice such capacities as self-control, frustration tolerance, and exploring their feelings with their caregivers.

How to Use This Workbook

There are several ways to use this workbook: as a guidance, reflection, and skill-building tool for parents; as a child-only activity; and as a parent-child activity that addresses emotion regulation with novelty and fun. In each parent guidance section there is a set of strategies listed that can be used to apply what you just learned or to deepen your understanding of the concept presented. Throughout this workbook you will see "real life examples" that come from our own lives or from other parents and caregivers that we know well. Additional information in outlined boxes will also give you more food for thought.

Book Structure

This book is for parents of children aged five to eight, as well as for children themselves. You may use this book in any way that is helpful to you. However, keep in mind that we have designed this book so that the WHY of good parenting is included in part 1 of the book. These are the foundational principles and concepts, including those backed by hundreds of research studies on child emotional functioning, on how children self-regulate. Reading this section alone will support your parenting skills. The HOW, part 2 of the book, includes discipline strategies designed to apply the essential principles and concepts. In order to get all of the things you really need (even the concepts you didn't know you needed), we recommend that you read (and reread!) through the foundational principles in the beginning of the book, as well as the strategies offered that support them. Part 3 is for parents and kids to use together, while part 4 is just for kids. Please offer to assist your younger child in using part 4 should they need support.

Imagination, Courage, Honesty

Using this workbook requires imagination, courage, and honesty.

Imagination

Allow your imagination to be one of your greatest parenting tools. Step into the world of your five- to eight-year-old child, and see the world from their eyes. When you use imagination as a parenting skill, it can help you to better understand your child's mind and interpret their behavior.

Courage

Take a baby step toward something new. If you find yourself "giving in" to a tough behavior because it seems to be the easier route, see what it's like to hold firm with a limit, even when it means your child will have a big reaction. If you have a hard time being silly, getting into character, playing a game or sport your child likes, again, take a step toward this shift with courage.

Honesty

Be in touch with the whole range and host of feelings you have about parenting your child. Radical honesty with yourself about your feelings toward parenting is essential to using this workbook well. Your child will benefit from your ability to be emotionally vulnerable.

Use the interventions on page 58 to support your use of imagination, courage, and honesty as a parent.

Your Unique Child

All children are unique—even identical twins. This book cannot and should not be "one size fits all." Some parts of this book may be challenging or seem too simple for your child. This is because this book is written for a range of ages, and there is a big difference between a five-year-old and an eight-year-old—the latter has been living almost twice as long! Children also vary in their capacities and how they develop. If your child is chronologically older than eight years old but functions with less emotional maturity in certain ways, you may also appreciate this book. If you are a teacher, caregiver to children, or therapist who works with parents and children, you will find the approaches offered in this book applicable in many settings. Parts of this workbook may feel accessible and just right for your child, and others may have to be grown into or modified in the ways you know best.

While it is completely normal for children to vary in their personalities, abilities, and capacities, another way they can differ is in their experiences. Children who have had big challenges in their early lives either because of poor early care, or perhaps medical issues, will likely have greater emotional challenges. This workbook is still appropriate for those children, but it may be that you will need additional help from specialists as well.

Why did I buy this workbook?

This might be a good time to reflect on why you have purchased this book! Please circle below the things that you are concerned about. We have listed the same things three times because it is always helpful to reflect back after a period of time and either see the progress you and your child have made, or perhaps note that you are stuck and could use some extra support from a professional.

I bought this book because I am worried about my child's (please circle as many as necessary):

Date:_____	Date:_____	Date:_____
Irritability	Irritability	Irritability
Tantrums	Tantrums	Tantrums
Rude behavior	Rude behavior	Rude behavior
Sadness	Sadness	Sadness
Ability to get along with others	Ability to get along with others	Ability to get along with others
Ability to function at school	Ability to function at school	Ability to function at school
Relationship with me	Relationship with me	Relationship with me
Self-esteem	Self-esteem	Self-esteem
Something else:_____	Something else:_____	Something else:_____

I bought this book because as a caregiver I would like to work on my:

Date:_____	Date:_____	Date:_____
Patience	Patience	Patience
Ability to connect with my child	Ability to connect with my child	Ability to connect with my child
Setting limits	Setting limits	Setting limits
Keeping a routine	Keeping a routine	Keeping a routine
Understanding my child's development	Understanding my child's development	Understanding my child's development
Enjoyment of parenting	Enjoyment of parenting	Enjoyment of parenting
Parent self-regulation	Parent self-regulation	Parent self-regulation
Something else:_____	Something else:_____	Something else:_____
_____	_____	_____

PART 1

THE "WHY" OF GOOD PARENTING

CHAPTER 1

FINDING YOUR CENTER
The Building Blocks of Child Self-Regulation

This section discusses the most important aspects of child self-regulation, those that are necessary for the development of this capacity in children. Many of these concepts come from our knowledge of emotion regulation during infant development. So much of what we did for our children from ages zero to three still applies for older children, just in a different form. Keeping these concepts at your center helps you to maintain your balance on the tightrope.

Attunement

Attunement is picking up on the nonverbal, subtle ways emotion shows up in yourself and others (Hughes 2009). These are times you are "in sync" with your child. Think: being able to "pick up" on cues of hunger or discomfort in a child, sharing in an experience of joy or sadness together, and "matching" the intensity of a child's emotional expressions. You pick up on what your child may feel through your history of tracking their facial expressions, vocal tone, and physical cues. You offer responses in tandem with their cues and underlying needs.

Attunement may also be explicit and expressive; it begins in infancy when a parent "mirrors" a sad or happy face, communicating their understanding of the infant's inner emotional state. This helps infants to better understand their own emotions as well as the range of responses to their emotion from their caregiver (Beebe and Steele 2013).

Attunement happens in micro moments between caregivers and children. We can see this demonstrated in the research of mothers and infants conducted by researcher Beatrice Beebe and her team. Her research shows patterns of attunement in micro moments of eye gaze, head turns, and facial expression. These patterns, those that form attachment security or insecurity, are set by four months of age (Beebe and Steele 2013). However, attachment patterns can change, including for children who may initially "resist" or have difficulty forming a secure attachment with foster or adoptive parents due to early trauma (Hughes 2009).

It's also perfectly fine and expected to be misattuned, or not "in sync" with your child at times. In studies on normal infant-caretaker communication, we have learned that healthy development is based on states that shift from mutually positive and well coordinated, to those that are miscoordinated and negative. These transitions from positive to negative, and vice versa, happen with great frequency, about once every three to five seconds. In other words, positive, coordinated interaction, when parent and baby are attuned, happen alongside frequent misattunement, and only about 30 percent of the time (Tronick 1989).

Fortunately, for us caregivers and parents, healthy child emotional development is not about being perfectly attuned at all times. It's more about seeking to *repair* misattunements and shift negative interactions to positive (more on the importance of repair soon). On a day-to-day basis, if we get it wrong the first time, we can try again. In fact, it is vitally important for us to get it wrong sometimes, as the "good enough" parent is meant to do. This is how we learn as parents. This is also how children learn, in micro ways, to emotionally "work through" the necessary missteps of their parent (Winnicott 1971).

Importantly, children learn how to attune to adults as well. To be able to "read" the parent is as important to their regulation as the parent being able to "read" the child (Beebe and Steele 2013). This is because children are dependent on their parents for their safety and their food and their everything! All healthy mammalian children are tuned in to their parents until they can meet their own needs. Think about adorable lambs following their mother sheep around the pasture. Attunement is bidirectional in nature: from parent to child and child to parent.

"My son and I were very attuned. Once when he was three and naturally climbing on every structure as I was hoping to get somewhere on time (and thinking about how slow he was!), he turned to me and said, 'Why do you have that sad face on, Mommy?'"

How do we better attune? Through working on our ability to be in the present moment with our children. We use our senses and our intuition; our eyes to observe our child's facial and bodily expressions; our hearing to pick up on shifts in their vocal tone and cadence, our touch to pick up on physical tension our child may be holding. With practice, being in sync can be one of the most natural and effortless things caregivers can do. Imagine the feel of dancing to the same beat, throwing a ball back and forth, walking at the same pace, etc. You are not exerting incredible effort to do those things, sometimes they just happen naturally.

We use attunement in moments that go below language, underneath behaviors, to connect with the feelings the child may be having in the moment. For example, even though your child declares they are "fine" after losing a game, you may pick up on their underlying feelings, and know to hold them closer. It's a particular language without words; you are interpreting nonverbal messages, as if you are translating from one language to another.

Attunement is emotional intimacy. The person who "can tell" when something is bothering you, who picks out the perfect gift for you, who can predict what you need and want—this person is highly attuned to you. Most of the time this can feel great. In the moment, it is a feeling of being seen, and of having your needs met, without having to spell it out.

Here are some questions to help you reflect on your attunement to your child:

How do you know when your child is upset?

→ Do they cry?

→ Do they whine?

→ Do they look red in the face?

→ Do they have a sad look?

→ Do they avoid eye contact?

Importantly, when we are adequately attuned to our child, we can notice early signs of dysregulation, and have a better opportunity to respond to their needs sooner rather than later. Over time, most parents become skilled at attuning to their child. So much so that it feels second-nature. However, it is harder to be in sync with someone else if you are caught up in your own problems or stress. It may also be hard to offer attunement to others if you haven't had enough of it in your own childhood or adult relationships. We'll address how to tend to your needs and care for yourself in order to be able to be an emotional support for your child, in further sections.

See "Playing with Attunement" (page 59) for more on how to experience attunement with your child.

Co-Regulation

How do we learn to soothe ourselves? None of us is born with this capacity. It starts from outside of us, with adequate responsiveness from a caregiver who tends to our distress. When this happens with enough consistency and care, the human infant learns that their states of hunger, sleep, fear, or other discomfort can be soothed by a safe, calm other. In this sense, our very first experience of self-regulation is provided through our relationship with our early caregivers (Midgley and Vrouva 2012; Slade 2023).

As a child matures, some aspects of self-regulation naturally develop. A child learns that their body and mind can calm down. They learn words to help organize and express their feelings; the act of communicating feelings can help regulate them. With enough experience of co-regulation, kids gain perspective, and lots of changes to the child's ability to process and recover from intense feelings can happen.

However, as your parenting experience thus far has likely shown you, *self-regulation in children requires a consistent experience of co-regulation with a trusted caregiver*. Children cannot self-regulate instinctively. It is a learned skill that requires repeated exposure from a trusted adult who is regulated themself.

Through co-regulation, parents of five- to eight-year-olds serve multiple roles:

→ As a container, helping kids pour out their big feelings and digest them, returning them in manageable pieces;

→ As a secure base for their child to have during an emotional storm, staying tethered to them;

→ As a coach supporting their child's ability to use their emerging emotion regulation skills, and keeping them physically safe.

These relational interactions are powerful and deep; they help to regulate a child's stress response system, putting into motion healing physiological states that are controlled by the brain (Ludy-Dobson and Perry 2010). As parents, we have access to our child's developing limbic systems, the part of the brain that mediates emotional learning and functioning (Tottenham 2023). This access is one of our many privileges and obligations as parents!

> Hundreds of research studies have illustrated the central role the caregiving relationship plays in the development of emotion regulation. Due to our very long period of brain development (more on that later!) parents scaffold emotional development, both in positive and potentially negative ways. A parent's calm presence can positively impact the child's physiological state, while a distressed or dysregulated parent can potentially activate a child's stress. In ideal circumstances, a child's stressful state can be buffered by the presence of a calm parent (Tottenham 2023).

When co-regulation is successful, the child eventually learns that they are not alone in having to manage big feelings, and as they age, they can gradually develop an internal sense of security about the possibility of being soothed. When a child can imagine the steady, loving presence of a parent, even at times when the parent is not available, this is their first rudimentary coping skill. They can then build on these skills.

More often than not, a child needs co-regulation before being able to talk about what's wrong or solve a problem. Their ability to use the parts of their brain that help them think about their emotions is compromised when they are dysregulated. They need co-regulation in order to bring back the capacity to think and begin to understand the emotions connected to their distress (Siegel and Bryson 2012). Through enough experiences of co-regulation, kids' bodies and brains learn that a big, intense, or upsetting feeling can get smaller over time.

Co-regulation is the process of soothing and regulating another person through a safe and loving relationship. It calms the nervous system and reduces stress. When we co-regulate, we are offering our calm and accepting presence to our child, and supporting their ability to get to a calmer state. Our calm is contagious; they gain it through osmosis.

It's Just So Important: More on Co-Regulation

Think of the last time you were really frustrated, sad, angry, or disappointed about something. Who calmed you down? Who didn't? Consider why or why not.

In general, we would like someone who makes us feel better, not worse; someone who does not overreact to the situation, who doesn't focus on their own feelings, or blame us for having our own. Someone who, at the very least, gives us their undivided attention. Ideally this person would be warm, curious about our feelings, and well-regulated themselves. This person would acknowledge our distress and use a soothing tone of voice. It's hard to imagine feeling calmed by someone who is also upset.

There are many ways to co-regulate, some of which will be explained in the interventions we recommend at the end of this section. For now, here is a simple list:

→ Offering eye contact and full presence
→ Coming down to your child's level and placing a hand on their chest
→ Listening without offering any advice
→ Staying calm yourself
→ Using mmmhhhs, and nodding your head

REAL-LIFE EXAMPLE

"On vacation after a long day, while trying to get to sleep in a strange bed, my six-year-old got very upset. I came by her side and gently patted her back with a quiet shush, shush sound until she was able to finish her 'crying talking' and fall asleep."

Parenting five- to eight-year-olds can trigger us in ways nothing else can! It's hard to offer co-regulation if you are annoyed with your child for being upset. Children this age get upset over so many little things that don't really matter in the long run. This kind of parenting stress can activate primitive parts of the brain that trigger fight, flight, or freeze responses. Just like kids, we can get overstimulated, feel thwarted or powerless, and melt down. As always, we try to do our best and give ourselves, and our children, grace. See our section on parent self-regulation for more support.

More Co-Regulation Interventions to Support Your Child

→ Co-Regulation with Words (page 95) and Co-Regulation without Words (page 96)
→ Sharing Stories (page 92)
→ Use of Validation for Child's Emotional Expressions (page 86)
→ HALT, Child Version (page 90)
→ Use of Physical Regulation (page 84)
→ Calm Bodies (page 85)

Parent Self-Regulation

Here's the rub: in order to be your child's co-regulator, you need to be calm enough yourself. As we know, this proves to be very difficult at times. Kids have the potential to disrupt our peace and our plans (even the ones that are centered around them), ignore us and do their own thing, and forget to do things they have been told and taught repeatedly. Feeling a loss of power and control can trigger anger and anxiety in a lot of us. Most of the time, once we notice this feeling emerging, we can pivot and attempt to regulate (Siegel and Bryson 2012). The key is catching this wave of emotion, and to trust that the best and desired outcome is for us to remain calm.

This workbook contains numerous strategies targeting parent self-regulation, those that support emotional awareness and help you modify emotional states. Until you are feeling regulated, you cannot help your child (put your oxygen mask on first!). In the situation on page 13, the six-year-old's mom was very capable because she was also on vacation and felt very well rested and happy! If you are chronically stressed, it may be more difficult to self-regulate. If this is your situation, it is even more important for you to develop a practice of calming and soothing yourself.

Our goal for self-regulation is to calm the impulse to act out or react in some way that may not be helpful. We want to calm ourselves down enough to consider our many options. We usually have a number of ways we can respond to an intense moment with our children; we need to self-regulate in order to consider these options.

One of the keys to self-regulation is self-monitoring. Developing a way to monitor your thoughts, feelings, and bodily sensations during a tough time with your child puts you in a very good position to regain control and focus on regulating yourself. This can come in many, many forms; we offer numerous brief strategies to better track your emotions and monitor your escalation, as well as regulate intense emotions in yourself, in this workbook. See Strategies for Parent Self-Regulation (chapter 8) for more on how to support yourself.

Regulation can involve a combination of approaches that soothe intensive thoughts, calm strong sensations in the body, and help you develop self-compassion as well as empathy for your child.

Mentalizing and Reflective Functioning

When your child says, "Pick me up, pick me up!" as you are holding your neighbor's baby, and you think, "Is he feeling jealous?" you are engaging in a concept called mentalizing, one of the most studied phenomena in the literature on parent-child emotional functioning. Mentalizing is the ability to understand that behavior is not random; it is based on an individual's feelings, intentions, needs, desires, and perceptions in the moment (Allen, Fonagy, and Bateman 2008). When we mentalize, it supports our ability to "make sense" of the behaviors of ourselves and others, and to imagine how someone else may feel. Being able to ascribe or guess at a reason for others' actions toward us is a supportive life skill. You can stop and wonder, what may be going on in that person's heart and mind that causes them to act this way? Such questions can support perspective taking, social skills, and empathy toward others (Midgley and Vrouva 2012).

When we talk about the concept of mentalizing in parenting, it refers to the parents' ability to hold their child's mental states in mind and is called "parental reflective functioning" (Slade 2005). Reflective functioning is a specific type of thinking, one where we focus on the inner life of our child (Hughes 2009). When parents engage in reflective functioning, they make an effort to look beyond their child's behavior (what's at the surface) to imagine what it expresses underneath (below the surface), including the child's thoughts, feelings, and difficulties in the moment. Here, we consider things from the child's point of view, keeping in mind that their perspective may be very different from our own. When parents mentalize in relation to their child's difficult behavior, their perception of what may be going on can deepen and change. We don't have to jump to conclusions and react to our child without considering their side of things; we can use this ability to help both ourselves and our child make sense of their reactions.

Mentalizing about your child's behavior offers you a wider range of responses to your child's upsets. You may find yourself responding differently to a "problem behavior" when you take a moment to actively reflect on your child's inner emotional world. When a confusing or complicated behavior can make sense to us, it helps us reduce stress and be more effective in our responses to our child. Here is an example of strong vs. less developed parental reflective functioning:

MENTALIZING YOUR CHILD'S BEHAVIOR

LESS DEVELOPED PARENTAL REFLECTIVE FUNCTIONING	STRONG PARENTAL REFLECTIVE FUNCTIONING
"What made him push his brother? He hates him for no good reason."	"What made him push his brother? What was he feeling inside? I wonder if it's because I had given his brother so much attention for winning the big game, especially after not seeing me all day long."

Just like attunement and self-regulation, mentalizing may be difficult to develop if one is in a state of chronic stress. Under those conditions, there is not enough emotional or mental "energy" to devote curiosity about one's own or others' underlying emotional states (Midgley and Vrouva 2012). When children or adults feel a sense of blame or shame, these can also limit mentalizing capacity; reflecting on our underlying feelings, intentions, or desires can simply feel too painful or overwhelming at these times. Alternatively, parents who model mentalizing can enhance a child's reflective capacity through supporting them in understanding their internal experience and how it is connected to their behavior.

Mentalizing is a self-reflective practice and an imaginative capacity. It helps us interpret our own behaviors as well as the behavior of others through being curious about mental states (Fonagy, Gergely, Jurist, and Target, 2002). When we engage in parental reflective functioning, we allow a broader window of understanding and responses to our child's behaviors.

A Little More on Mentalizing

Yes, behavior has meaning.

Behaviors can be an expression of underlying emotions the child is feeling but not able to put into words. These behaviors may also be driven by their goals and underlying needs. They may "act out" things that are bothering them by showing behaviors that call our attention or are challenging to understand and support. When we have questions like "I wonder why he..." or "What on earth caused her to..." we are engaging in parental reflective functioning, a process that helps us figure out what may be driving our child's behaviors.

Kids may have mixed feelings about growing up that they cannot articulate and that they may not be aware of. This can be especially exacerbated if a new sibling comes along, or at the beginning or end of a transition from one stage to another. Kids may hear or see things that are normal to adults but that may scare or confuse them.

Adults, in turn, may take for granted that kids are learning certain things about life for the first time, things that may set off a series of questions, feelings, and concerns.

REAL-LIFE EXAMPLE

"I remember when my son was first exposed to the concept of being an orphan, around age six. There were many characters in the stories we read or movies we watched, from *Oliver the Musical*, to *Harry Potter*, to *Annie*, to *Bambi*. The idea that a kid could lose one or both parents seemed to rock him. He did not put this into words, of course, but instead he started to develop more separation issues at night. Because I was able to link these newer anxieties to the exposure my son had, I could have more empathy and less frustration with him during these moments."

Behavior has layers of meaning, ranging from the simple (a child is tired and overstimulated and breaks down in response to small stressors) to the complex (a child who feels shame and anger about the fact that they broke their favorite toy then acts out toward the parent trying to soothe them). As complex as behavior may be to unpack, parents can figure this out through expressing interest, observing their child, and using their own imaginations (Sorenson 2005). Being curious about what your child is communicating through their behavior is the best place to start.

For more, see Sometimes It's Not Just about the Goodie Bag on page 39.

More Interventions on Understanding and Interpreting the WHY Underneath Child Behaviors

→ Is This a Developing Skill? (page 70)

→ Zoom Out (page 67)

More Resources on Mentalizing with Your Child

→ Can You Imagine? (page 117)

→ Just For Kids section: I Know Who I Am (page 138); Would You Rather? (page 140)

When Things Go Wrong: Repair

Good parents have so much on their minds and on their to-do lists. They can miss their child's bids for attention or support, misread what they may need in the moment, or be delayed in their offering of the soothing, attention, or support their child needs. They can even (gasp!) react in a mean or unpleasant way at times. What we know from studies on attachment is that in securely attached relationships, it is not the avoidance of the mistakes that matters the most, but the effort to repair that matters (Hughes 2009). When the parent consistently repairs the relationship following the mistake, perceived rejection, or lack of sensitivity, the relationship can actually deepen. This is because the experience of rupture and repair allows the child to experience an important truth: that despite whatever big or small errors the parent makes in the moment and the hurts that causes, the relationship is always able to return to a state of loving connection and understanding. This truth offers security to both the parent and child, one that is crucial to the maintenance of secure attachment.

How do we repair? First, you can self-reflect: What about this behavior made me lose my cool? What is happening for me that created this strong reaction? Can I give myself some empathy for not being able to show up as my best parent self?

Then, you act like an adult: You acknowledge how your response affected your child (perhaps you were hurtful, overly harsh, or wrong) or made the situation worse, and you apologize. Importantly, you can acknowledge that you got frustrated or angry for good reason, but that you got *too* angry (Barish 2012). You might say, "I'm sorry I snapped at you. I had a tough day at work. I shouldn't have taken it out on you."

Why May It Be Hard to Apologize to a Child?

Many reasons! You have to be self-aware enough to admit to a wrong-doing, intentional or not. You have to process the shame, guilt, or sadness you may be holding about this misstep, and that is hard. You may never have been apologized to by your own parents. You may believe that children do not deserve an apology, that it upsets the balance of power in the relationship. Also, apologizing itself can feel awkward! You may not know what to say, and it may make you feel emotional. Despite all of this discomfort, the truth is, parents have a lot more to gain than they have to lose from acknowledging a mistake or overreaction.

The act of repairing is not about buying something for your child, or allowing a treat to make up for your loud voice or being cranky, it is about sincerely apologizing. Here is an inexhaustive list of how many parents (even good ones) avoid repairing:

→ Come check on child after a fight but don't apologize

→ Serve an unexpected snack or dessert

→ Offer to help with something they normally don't

→ Buy a gift for a child

→ Be overly nice, sweet, or calm in some way, to "make up" for their harshness

→ Simply acting like the fight/upset didn't happen; pretending everything is normal

→ What would you add to this list, that either you or your own parent has done?

These are not repairs. They are gestures that signal to a child that the threat is over, but they do not address the underlying feelings and potential unmet emotional needs of a child. There is an elephant in the room that leaves both you and your child feeling uncomfortable.

What you lose in withholding apologies is much greater than what you and your child may gain. When you withhold you lose out on a modeling opportunity for your child, showing them an example of when and how to apologize to someone. You also lose showing your child something true, vulnerable, and real about you and your humanity. You lose the opportunity to protect a child from internalizing something negative about themselves (I am a bad kid/my hurt feelings do not deserve attention/when someone does something wrong to me, they do not need to be held accountable, etc.). Again, there is so much more that can go wrong in withholding an apology than in offering one.

One of the main benefits in offering a repair is that it supports parent regulation. Offering a repair is a way to address the tension and stress you are carrying yourself. You can say, "I've done the best I can" to remedy the situation. You can feel connected to your child again, one of your most important attachment relationships. Your child learns that everyone makes mistakes sometimes; what a deeply important life lesson! It teaches children that you can still be loved even when you've made a mistake.

When your feelings are hurt and someone acknowledges their part in it, it doesn't make the feelings magically disappear, but it does support the healing of the hurt. A repair is an emotional Band-Aid: just as you would not ignore a cut on your child's body for fear that it could grow worse, you would not want to ignore their hurt feelings.

We'd like to argue that making a repair is an important display of authority, not a sign of weakness. Adults take accountability for their actions. Adults take responsibility to fix a problem they may have caused. Emotionally mature people consider the impact of their actions on others. When you've had a boss that has messed something up and not acknowledged their mistake, do you respect them less or more? How about a boss who is transparent about a mistake and delineates a plan of action to prevent it from happening in the future? How do you feel toward them then?

Repairing sends kids the message that their hurt feelings are deserving of care. Ideally this supports their sense of self, so they can then walk around the world feeling dignified and deserving of care from others.

Repairs require *bravery*. If you have never apologized to someone or never had an apology offered to you, this may feel scary and unknown. You may not feel at your best. You may feel weak and unsure. Here, you can also use your imagination. Think of someone you know, a character from a book or movie or family member you admire. How would they offer a repair?

REAL-LIFE EXAMPLE

"Coming home from a long car ride, I was exhausted and dealing with a recurring back injury. All I wanted was some peace and quiet. My daughter had different ideas. As I walked into the kitchen to get a glass of water, she followed me in. She wanted to be near me, dawdle, and chat before getting her pajamas on and getting into bed (it was past her bedtime, at that). I was frustrated, tired, and in pain. I could barely put into words what I was feeling, but said something like, 'I really need space!' and shooed her away impatiently with my hands, as though she were a pest. I could see the pained look on her face as she walked away mumbling something about wanting to give me a hug. As she walked out of the kitchen, I knew it was not my finest moment, and that when I felt a bit better, I would follow up.

"When I calmed my own irritation, I let my daughter know that I was sorry I shooed her away. I let her know that I was not feeling well and then gave her a hug. This brought us back to a place of balance."

Further examples of when a repair can feel clearly warranted, and in short order (that is, only after the parent themselves has regulated and feels able to offer an authentic repair that is brief, direct, and warm):

→ When you promised something and you mistakenly didn't do that thing

→ When you yell or punish overly harshly

→ When you cause your child to feel hurt, shame, or embarrassment

→ When you speak badly of others or put your child in a position to see or hear things that they shouldn't

→ When you blame your child unfairly

→ When you break, lose, or forget something important to them

The list can go on.

REAL-LIFE EXAMPLE

"Once after returning from a vacation, I found a quilt that I had made in the laundry basket covered in wet towels, which caused it to start to mold. I was so angry! I said, 'Who did this?!' When my son fessed up, I didn't shout but I was just beside myself and I am sure he felt it as I told him that you can't leave wet towels in a clump for days on end. The level of my anger was a mystery even to me, until I realized that I was still upset about the vacation we had taken to visit my sister. She hadn't been easy to get along with, and I was disappointed that we had gone rather than just spending time as a small family. Once I understood this, I was able to tell my son that I was upset about something else, and that it wasn't such a big deal—mistakes happen. I let him know that I was sorry I seemed so angry."

Here are some simple steps to guide a repair:

→ Notice when you have calmed enough and have started to process your anger, shame, or guilt.

→ Consider what you would like to say to your child.

→ Say "I'm sorry" and link the apology to your poor response.

→ Offer a hug, high five, or back rub, if accepted.

→ Offer your child a chance to respond and share how they feel.

→ Be brief! Try not to talk too much or you may end up overexplaining, mistakenly blaming the child, making excuses, etc.

→ Notice: are you often having to make repairs? And if so, why?

It's okay if it takes you some time to apologize. A golden rule: apologies are better late than never. A late apology can even reflect how much you were thinking about or bothered by the stressful episode and how important it is to let your child know you care.

Are there things you can repair, and things you can't? This is an important question. Repairs are always warranted when you've really lost yourself as a parent, but recurring parent anger, blow-ups, or ignoring your child's emotional needs require true behavioral change and a commitment to work towards getting it right. In this case, as a parent, you may want to consider getting more help for yourself as it concerns these recurring issues.

More Interventions on Repairing with Your Child

CHAPTER 2

CAREGIVER-CHILD CONNECTION
The Heart of Child Self-Regulation

Nourishing the relationship with your child and providing a loving environment full of opportunities to connect, laugh, and enjoy each other's presence feeds the well of relational safety that allows kids to thrive. Their feeling unconditionally loved by you is a baseline for their own self-regulation. When your child feels connected to you, they are more motivated to cooperate and be flexible; they enjoy that good feeling of being in connection, and strive to maintain it. A positive connection allows children to make better use of their own brains and your support in managing and recovering from upsets (Siegel and Bryson 2012). Connection feeds a child's inner sense of goodness and lovability; through their connection they can more easily recover from upsets and return to a state of calm.

Luckily for us, there are so very many ways to connect, big and small, even in a matter of seconds or minutes. In this section, we highlight the role of connection through play, as five- to eight-year-olds love to play.

Connection through Play

Play is our child's love language! Imagine someone asking you to talk about your favorite movie or book, allowing you to speak freely, while they listen attentively and ask more questions. Or accompanying you on an activity that you love, allowing you to share it with them. For our kids, this boosts their serotonin, our brain's love and connection neurotransmitter.

Play serves another very important purpose: especially in imaginative play, kids get to feel bigger, stronger, and more capable. This is a nourishing feeling. Another benefit: fantasy play with characters can support the development of a child's emotional reflection and expression. With the help of parents, kids can become curious about a character, including asking questions and making observations. This allows kids to imagine why people do what they do.

As simple as it may be to play with a child, adults may find play boring, annoying, or frustrating. We may have a set of necessary tasks to take care of and little free time. We may not have been played with ourselves, or our current life circumstances may not feel very playful at all. However, playing with your child, phone-free, with as much attention and engagement as you can muster, has many advantages for you and your relationship with your child.

Many five-year olds love to engage in child-led, collaborative play, while six- to eight-year-olds are beginning to play with rules and feel excited to keep track of scores (Tyson and Tyson 1990). When you are short on time, energy, or patience to engage in an activity that is more time consuming, here are some ideas for squeezing in play time with your five- to eight-year-old.

Suggestions for 5 to 15 minutes of play time:

→ Games for short blasts of fun: Uno, Go Fish, Spot it, Eye Found It, Connect 4, Candyland, The Floor Is Lava, Hangman, Tic-Tac-Toe

→ Puzzles (set a timer for 15 minutes)

→ Jenga

→ Mother May I

→ Make up a story. Ask your child to name an object, a color, and a letter and use these elements to make up a story.

→ Read from a book of jokes or riddles.

→ Pretend play with dolls or toys.

→ Show and Tell

→ Charades/Animal Charades

→ Freeze dance: Dance to one to three high-energy, favorite songs.

→ Basketball (set a timer or make it best of five), tossing a ball

→ Blow bubbles and try to keep them up in the air/make the biggest bubble.

→ Draw together (squiggle game, exquisite corpse; see page 134 for details).

→ Hand-clapping games (Have your child teach you the latest ones!)

→ Read a favorite book.

→ Head's Up (as a card game or with your cell phone)

→ Two truths and a lie

→ Simon Says

→ ABC Scavenger Hunt

When engaging in pretend play with your child, allow your child to lead it: ask for their suggestions on what characters do or say, ask questions about the characters, be emotionally responsive to the narrative elements, and make observations. See if you can explore together what the characters and their motives are all about, including how they may feel. Avoid asking overly academic or clarifying questions and allow for fantasy elements that do not have to make sense.

When our kids have grown to this stage of childhood, we may find ourselves with more options than we had before for enjoying time as a family (Novick and Novick 2010). Kids are becoming more self-sufficient and their own networks are growing. So, the gift of this age: parents do not always have to choose between what will make the child happy versus what will make the adult happy. Can you find some activities where adults and children can both enjoy? Consider your options for family fun that are not exclusively child-driven.

REAL-LIFE EXAMPLE

"My summer favorite is an outdoor picnic at the local park. I bring a speaker to play music, balls to throw around, and drinks and snacks, then enjoy the sun on a beautiful day, playing on and off with the kids."

More Interventions to Connect with Your Child

→ Filling the Well (page 82)

→ Increasing Empathy (page 64)

CHAPTER 3

THE IMPORTANCE OF MODELING

Sometimes It Feels Like Somebody's Watching Me...

How would you feel if your child repeated you, word for word, in your most stressed and frustrated moments? When we show our ability to be flexible and recover from things like making a mistake, not getting something we want, or struggling with a task, it gives our kids a sense that this is possible and provides a model.

REAL-LIFE EXAMPLE

"My sister is a really good baker. One Thanksgiving I was making pies and somehow all of the fillings leaked to the bottom and cemented the crust to the pans. I was so disappointed! I felt like throwing them all in the garbage. Instead, I said, 'Oh no! This is so disappointing. My sister would never have let this happen!' My kids laughed and repeat this last phrase to this day. On that day, they said, 'We can eat them anyway!'"

What do you want to model for them? How did *you* learn to express frustration, state preferences, and allow for sadness? This section discusses the incredible importance of modeling emotion regulation and expression for your children, so that they can see an example of how to do it themselves. Just as we would not expect a child to begin to talk, read, or ride a bike without anyone ever teaching them how to, we cannot expect children to develop a skill as complex as emotion regulation if they have never seen their parents display it themselves.

It's important to model things small and big, and to voice your internal monologue. If your child refuses to try new foods, it's important to show them that you can try something you've never had before. If your child refuses to have play dates with other kids, show them the importance of spending time with friends by doing it yourself. If your child has difficulty expressing their emotions, talk about and express emotions yourself.

You want to model emotional expression, resilience, and flexibility. This does not mean you put on a happy face when you are really upset or hide when you have big emotions. It means showing your child that there are ways to support yourself when you are upset, as well as how you recover from upsets. What we want kids to see is that emotions come and go, and that when they come, we can feel them and recover from them. One way you can model emotional expression is through shared experiences. For example, during a movie or sports game, you can say, "I was so nervous at that part, I wasn't sure if the hero would win!" You can cry when you feel moved by something you see or hear: "This song is so touching, it always brings a tear to my eye." You can get upset on someone else's behalf: "I'm frustrated that no one else offered a seat to that elderly woman on the bus!"

REAL-LIFE EXAMPLE

"I recently lost a piece of jewelry from my grandmother that I always wore. After searching for it all over the house and realizing it might truly be lost, I expressed my upset feelings aloud. I said something like, 'Losing this necklace is so upsetting to me. I am so disappointed and sad about this. All I can do is hope that it turns up one day.' I then eventually moved on to another task, still a little downtrodden. Soon after, I started wearing a new necklace that I loved, even without the sentimental value. When I found the necklace I lost a few weeks later, my daughter was so happy for me and cheered, knowing how hard it was to experience that temporary loss."

More Interventions to Model Emotional Resilience with Your Child

→ Feel Your Escalation (page 60)

→ Move the Goal Post (page 64)

→ Planned Ignoring (page 68)

→ Naming and Noticing Feelings (page 92)

→ Parent Self-Regulation for Intensive Situations (page 99)

Creating an Internal Sense of Self and Others

So what does parenting do, all the time, in the calm and stormy phases? For our children, we are helping them form an internal sense of themselves and others, a template from which they will interpret later relationships and experiences. We call these "internal working models" and they are powerful predictors of a child's later emotional functioning and functioning in relationships (Bowlby 1973). All of the thousands of interactions we have with our children create a sense of a child's inner sense of themselves, including their goodness and lovability. A child internalizes a sense of self in part through our adult responses: when an adult delights in their company, "I am delightful," when an adult listens intently to a child's story, "I am interesting," etc.

The Curious Case of the "Bad Kid"

"He's a bad kid." Have you ever thought this toward a child, or heard someone else say it? When kids have an internal sense that adults expect them to be "bad," something curious happens—they act the part! This may occur for many reasons, some of them being unconscious to the child. If children feel they will be labeled negatively and that this label could come from some adult at any point, they may unconsciously seek to take "control" of this dynamic by first acting out themselves. That's because it always feels better to kids to have a sense of control, rather than this rebuke happening randomly. This is especially true for kids who have experienced harm.

In our practices, we have found that reflecting on a child's inner goodness and lovability, including ALL of the unique things to notice about them (Example: How they think, their likes and pet peeves, etc.) can help remind them that they are whole, complete, complex people, not just "bad" or "difficult." What are their interests? How do they see the world?

Decades of research have revealed the potential impact of poor parent-child relationships on our life outcomes. Offering our children warmth and affection matters. Children who do not receive sufficient emotional care grow into adults who have to work harder to believe that they deserve love and care. If you are one of those adults, part of your own healing journey involves doing for your kids what you didn't have yourself.

There is cultural variation in using words of affirmation and affection in parenting. People can still feel deeply loved by their parents, even in the absence of hearing the words "I love you." However, just as in making repairs, we see more benefit in pushing yourself to express your feelings of connection and care in all ways, including explicitly with words, than not.

More Interventions to Create a Positive Internal Sense of Self with Your Child

→ Use of Praise and Connected Praise (page 72)

→ Use of Connected Rewards (page 73)

→ Filling the Well (page 82)

→ Increasing Empathy (page 64)

CHAPTER 4

SCOPING THINGS OUT
Important Developmental Factors

Here we discuss what to reasonably expect from children this age in terms of their self-regulation capacity.

A Day in the Life of a Child's Brain

Imagine going through a day at your job or with your family not being able to accurately predict the consequences of a present action or not being able to inhibit socially unacceptable responses. On this day you would have a really difficult time suppressing urges, and you may blurt out things you may later regret (this meeting is *boring*!). It would be harder to plan things out, make decisions, and differentiate good from bad (Dorito and pickle sandwiches anyone?). This would be a day in the life with an immature prefrontal cortex, the part of our brain that is not fully developed until adulthood, which mediates these functions (Siegel and Bryson 2012).

Are They Doing It on Purpose?

From studying human development, we know that the brain takes incredibly long to mature fully. In fact, human beings have the longest childhood of any species on earth (Gopnik 2016). Through these studies we know the structures of the brain that have the most to do with emotion regulation and executive functions (remembering rules, planning, organizing, and inhibiting impulses) mature the latest, not until we are considered adults. Because their brains are immature, we know that most five- to eight-year-olds are still learning how to control impulses and put their feelings into words, among other coping skills. Simply put, developmentally speaking, a child cannot have the same capacity to regulate strong emotions as an adult. We adults know this intrinsically, but at times, we need to be reminded.

"The immature brain is not a miniature brain—it is designed to do what it is supposed to do at that developmental moment in time." (Tottenham 2023)

At five to eight years old a child's brain is undergoing a "pruning" stage, becoming more efficient at functions like problem solving and decision making, that which is uniquely tailored to the environment they live in. Now that they have shown this incredible growth, it may tempt us to believe that kids can perhaps be better emotional managers of themselves. However, in reality, they still have *about 20 years to go* until their ability to plan, inhibit emotional responses, and predict consequences are mature.

How to use this information to support empathy and be realistic:

→ **Remind:** Because kids this age may have difficulty keeping rules in mind, they need reminders.

→ **Stay consistent:** They are not forgetting things on purpose; kids need repeated exposure to internalize rules and expectations. Caregivers have to stay as consistent as possible as kids' brains benefit from repetition.

→ **Be prepared:** Your child will fall apart sometimes. When a child is dysregulated (shouting, throwing, hitting, tantruming), it's not always because they want to or are trying to. Their ability to control the impulses that trigger these behaviors is limited.

→ **Be aware:** The frontal lobes are the parts of the brain that support development of emotion regulation skills. They mature over time. Importantly, they also mature through being used actively. This means it is important not only to be aware of your child's vulnerabilities, but also to support their growth (see section on Strengthening Adaptive Skills and the Ability to Self-Regulate on page 52).

→ **Use those muscles:** When you have observed, on many occasions, that your child has the "emotional muscles"(Novick and Novick 2010) to regulate emotion in a particular situation, you can calmly and gently remind them:

- I've seen you wait your turn.
- You are great at handling frustration like this.
- You can do this, just like the last few times.

Big Things Affect Little Brains

Chronic stress (such as exposure to trauma or neglect, including poverty) changes the architecture of little brains (Scientific Council on the Developing Child 2015). We know from decades of research that these experiences can have lifelong impacts, as the five- to eight-year-old period is still considered a "sensitive" period of development (for more on the impact of adversity in early childhood, see the ACES study; Felitti et al. 1998). Kids' brains benefit from routine and predictability, so it is important to give kids extra support and attention when their routine is going to be thrown off or needs to be adjusted in some major way. Not all change is traumatic, of course, but kids do benefit from age-appropriate support as it concerns separation/divorce, moving, loss, or upsetting events in their communities and in the news. Although kids do not always react the way adults do to such events, it's not true that they just don't feel anything at all. They may not talk about their feelings directly but they may act them out, or have some mild or noticeable regression in their functioning. Take care to support your child when life circumstances are going to impact them in some way. Set yourself up as the model for emotional expression and regulation, as a reliable source of information, and a safe place to turn to during life's ups and downs.

More Interventions to Keep Your Child's Development in the Forefront of Your Mind

→ Is This a Developing Skill?? (page 70)

→ Practice Makes Progress (page 77)

→ Zoom Out (page 67)

→ Increasing Empathy (page 64)

→ Use of Praise and Connected Praise (page 72)

CHAPTER 5

BEYOND BASICS
Beginning to Walk the Tightrope

This section covers aspects of parenting and child self-regulation that greatly enhance the basic capacities we covered in the previous sections. Read on to further develop your tightrope walking skills.

Don't Hold In a Sneeze

It is important to feel feelings, and to feel them fully. Generally speaking, a good sneeze can be relieving; the tension that builds up is released, and we can breathe more clearly. Sometimes, a healthy, robust sneeze just needs to take over. We can apply this same principle to the expression of feelings in children. There is a deep importance to the full-bodied, complete, and utter expression of feelings in children.

One of the best ways for kids to learn to regulate their feelings is to feel them. They have to get to know the felt-sense of these feelings, in their bodies and their minds, in order to learn how to deal with and recover from them. The more they get to know the intensity of these waves of emotion, the better they can become at learning their shape, depth, and the map back to shore. If this learning gets cut off prematurely by a child being told they shouldn't or can't have the full wave of their feelings, they may have a harder time learning how to better handle the full intensity of them. Think of an adult you know who was never allowed to be angry, or told that it's "weak" to cry. When they have these feelings as an adult, it can feel paralyzing and destabilizing, as opposed to known and manageable.

Feeling your feelings is a most important skill for life; when you feel capable of facing the intensity of your feelings, you learn that you can tolerate them, that they won't last and won't hurt you. As adults we know the only way to feel all the way better about something that bothers you is to allow yourself to feel your feelings and deal with them, rather than to avoid them or stuff them down.

When our children have one of these waves, we need to rely on our inner steadiness, an anchor inside of us that is not able to be swept away. This anchor is our Parent self-regulation, allowing us to practice non-reactivity and to consider our options for co-regulation. This means that sometimes you will need to be a lighthouse for your child's storms—not disrupting, or interrupting, but a steady, pulsating, calming presence. We support with the calm, immovable silence of a lighthouse. Our gaze and "mmm hmms" will allow our child to move closer to their own shores, slowly and steadily. Or, you may also imagine yourself as a flagpole, and your child's emotions are a flag in the wind. Your job is to stand firm, offering a stable, secure base for your child to remain tethered to. During an emotional storm, another option is to choose to be physically present but stay focused on you, and regulating yourself. After all, one way to define "success" when it comes to responding to our child's emotional upsets is our ability to stay calm throughout.

There are many times when allowing this wave of emotion in children to run its natural course will feel frustrating or unnecessary. That our children are crying over "nothing" or for "no good reason." There are even some professionals who agree with this notion, who advise that it is best to insist and actively assist a child in calming down. In some cases, that may be necessary (children are complex and parenting calls for different things at different times). However, we have found in practice that in most cases, allowing a child to ride out a wave of feeling, while offering co-regulation, can often be the most efficient way to resolve emotional upset and allow a child to fully bounce back.

Finally, the most important reason to allow children to feel feelings fully is because this may be an opportunity for your child to release pent-up feelings about hurts and upsets they have been holding in all day, all week, or all month! They may not even be all that upset about the thing they are upset about, but it's the "straw that broke the camel's back." Here, the dam breaks and they don't have to hold back anymore; they can have the healthy cry they didn't even know they needed.

See more about the importance of this in Sometimes It's Not Just about the Goodie Bag on page 39.

Wave? This Is a Tsunami!

When we can intervene early enough in a brewing storm, it can really help to clear it out. However, when our child's emotional waves feel more like a tsunami, we guide and soothe our child to smoother sailing waters. These times, we act like the Coast Guard, aiding our kids out of dangerously choppy seas. We offer our voice, our body, our empathy. We throw out a rope and a buoy.

This can look and sound like:

→ Getting down to your child's level and making eye contact

→ Using as soothing and calming a tone as possible

→ Being as warm as you can

→ Staying patient, calm, and firm about physical boundaries

→ Using phrases such as:

- It's okay to feel sad.
- We can handle this.
- I've got you.
- Let's get you a drink of ice water.
- I know you are very upset. Let's sit on the couch together.
- I have room for you right here on my lap.

Through these actions we build on the child's experience of finding calm and connection after a storm.

More Interventions on Allowing Feelings to Run Their Natural Course in Your Child

→ Co-Regulation with Words (page 95)

→ Co-Regulation without Words (page 96)

→ Help Children Talk about Their Feelings (page 91)

→ Use of Validation for Child's Emotional Expressions (page 86)

More Interventions to Support Your Child's Emotional Tsunami

→ Handling Outbursts in Public Spaces (page 97)

→ Calm Bodies (page 85)

→ Parent Self-Regulation for Intensive Situations (page 99)

→ How to Help Your Body Deal with Big Emotions (for Kids) (page 129)

→ HALT, Child Version (page 90)

→ Use of Physical Regulation (page 84)

A Story about Disappointment, from 8 to 81 Years Old

When the restaurant ran out of their famous potato salad, the one that my mother-in-law was looking forward to for her birthday dinner, she expressed mild frustration and disappointment, and ordered the sweet potatoes instead. She then complained to a family member or two about this upset, and was even considering calling the restaurant the next day to further complain. Think about the set of complex emotional skills required to manage such an experience; it's harder than it sounds.

Let's put this in contrast to an eight-year-old, who earlier that day refused to say good-bye to her best friend because she was so disappointed about the color of the gift bag she received following a very fun birthday party. Sullen, with arms crossed, she "rudely" ignored her friend's lovely wave and smile good-bye. The feelings of frustration had overpowered her ability to do the "right" thing. Instead, what felt right to her at the time was to protest and express her agitation, despite how it might have impacted others. For an eight-year-old, it would have been absolutely unnatural, and incredibly challenging, to politely button this feeling up and quickly move on to the next best goodie bag. It's just not how it works in a child's brain or body.

As adults, we clearly understand that a child cannot handle the same feeling—whether that be one of disappointment, frustration, or fear—in the ways that an adult can. However, in our tougher parenting moments, it is easy to forget this. We adults have developed a generally reliable road map to help us feel and deal with these emotions. We've also gained a perspective on what is important in life and what is not, to know that in life, there are ups and downs, wins and losses. We have a sense of what feelings and experiences are temporary versus forever. If we get good enough at it, we have learned not to sweat the small stuff. Of course, even as adults, this is not always easy to do.

To help our own internal steadiness when it comes to our child's disappointment about the small stuff, it is a good exercise to recall what it's like to experience a great disappointment as a child. Here are some pretty universally disappointing experiences we've had as children.

As you read them, see what it's like to notice your visceral reactions:

→ The agony of a balloon slipping out of your grip, watching it slowly fly away.

→ The frustration and despair of having an ice cream scoop fall off the top of the cone right on to the dirty sidewalk.

→ The fear and discomfort of being in line with your classmates, waiting to be picked for a team.

The list can go on and on. What's it like to remember these feelings in your body? What sensations do they stir up? What other memories and associations are you having?

We may also forget how big positive feelings are too; a five- to eight-year-old can have whole-bodied excitement about small things, enjoy life's most simple pleasures, and get completely enveloped in positive sensations. Here are just a few examples:

→ Swinging high in a swing, with the wind rushing through you.

→ Seeing your parent at the end of your school day.

→ Being snuggled in your own bed with your favorite stuffed animals.

It is normal for five- to eight-year-olds to feel big, big feelings in both directions. It's part of being a child.

For more on this topic see Amazing Kids on page 102.

How Do Children Process Tough Emotions, and What Is Our Role in It?

Loss, disappointment, frustration, anger, jealousy, sadness. When it comes to supporting our children through their storms, we have many options. And we will need them all, at some point or another. As is the nature of our evolving child, one approach may work beautifully one day while the same approach could send you flying off the tightrope another day.

Let's continue our example about disappointment about the eight-year-old and her goodie bag.

Focus on behavior: "You are being so rude! Get it together and say good-bye to your friend!"

Focus on emotions: "This is such a tough feeling! You are so upset!"

Focus on both: "You are so disappointed that you did not get what you wanted! That is a tough feeling." *[pause and let that soak in]* "And, when our friends say good-bye, it's important to say good-bye back because it may hurt our friends' feelings otherwise."

Focusing on the feelings *along with* the behavior helps a child's main problem in that moment, their internal storm.

Importantly, when your child lacks a coping skill for dealing with a feeling (in this case, disappointment, frustration, and feeling left out), you can teach this coping skill. You could say: "The next time you are feeling this way and it feels too hard to say good-bye, you could:"

1. Ask me to wave for you.

2. Just give a head nod or say good-bye through the window.

3. Follow up with your friend afterwards with a nice note.

Add your own example from a recent experience of your own:

This happened... _____

_____

_____

_____

Focus on behavior: _____

_____

_____

Focus on feelings: _____

_____

_____

Focus on both: _____

_____

_____

Offer a way of coping with this in the future: _____

_____

_____

When we focus on both feelings and behaviors, kids eventually learn that we care about both, not just one or the other. Over time, they can learn to better connect what feelings may be driving certain behaviors. In our own responses, we stay nimble, adapting in the moment to best support the needs of our child.

> Part of our adaptation depends on how much gas we have in our parenting tanks. We may do less in terms of empathy, guidance, and setting limits when we are low on gas.

More Related Interventions

→ Co-Regulation with Words (page 95)

→ Co-Regulation without Words (page 96)

→ Increasing Empathy (page 64)

→ Use of Validation for Child's Emotional Expressions (page 86)

Sometimes It's Not Just about the Goodie Bag: More on What's Underneath Child Behaviors

When we are upset about something, what would happen if we were allowed to speak freely, without any criticism or directive to stop? If someone invited us to tell them more as they listened intently, with warmth? We often find that our feelings about the "small things" can reflect deeper concerns or upsets (Wipfler and Schore 2016).

In the previous example when the 8-year-old girl did not say good-bye to her friend and sullenly left the birthday party, her parent cooled off enough to offer her some empathy and support. Her parent mostly moved out of the way of this emotional wave, allowing it to run its course, without disruption or interruption from a disapproving or critical adult. In this way, this girl was able to fully express herself, and as it turns out, her upset feelings were *not* just about the goodie bag.

As we discussed earlier, in our section about allowing a child to have their wave of emotion, sometimes your child will be upset about the goodie bag. But sometimes the goodie bag is just the break in the dam, allowing for a flood of other feelings, some of them buried just under the surface. This is, in fact, not a bad thing. This girl did not get the color goodie bag she wanted. As her parent allowed her the room to express herself, more of her important feelings came through: she was a few minutes late to the party so she had to be in the back of the room, not near her close friend; when it came time to break a board (this was a karate party), she was the only one in the party that took three tries to break it; when the goodie bags were brought out, her friend announced "ooh, the purple ones!" and all the kids within earshot grabbed up the prized color before she even got a chance. A series of upsets and disappointments, followed by a whopper. In total, her upset feelings made more sense: she felt really left out. From this place her parent could offer more genuine care, comfort, and soothing of her child's upset feelings.

When someone else hears our "full story," the reason behind our upset feelings, they are in a better position to offer empathy.

Just like my mother-in-law with her disappointment about the potato salad, it's important to share with kids that all people get upset and disappointed, and it is a normal feeling to have.

More Interventions on Allowing Emotions to Flow and Going Underneath Upset Feelings

→ Use of Validation for Child's Emotional Expressions (page 86)

→ Help Children Talk about Their Feelings (page 91)

Kids Are Supposed to Misbehave

We have all been there, each one of us. We've refused to do what someone asked, or done the opposite. We've pretended we didn't hear what they said. We've protested a command, dug in our heels, and said, "No!" In fact, you may recall an experience as an adult where you didn't do the thing expected of you, and perhaps just because you didn't want to!

Children are especially designed to misbehave at times. This is because they are learning so much, in real time, about rules and expectations and about their level of power and control in relation to others. They are impulsive and are not always able to maintain self-control. They don't want to stop playing when asked, because playing is fun! They don't want to hurry up and get their shoes on to leave for school, because they really want to see how far they can launch their Cheerio from their spoon. They usually have uniquely different priorities from adults, and are unaware of how time elapses and what is required in a chain of events, such as going out of the door on a snowy day. They are seeking to understand boundaries and limits, and their brains need repeated exposure to these limits in order to learn them. In other words, kids are supposed to ignore and break rules, push limits, and refuse adult commands. It is a healthy and normal behavior, and for many kids, an antidote to feeling small in the world.

Thoughts on Discipline and Punishment

So how are we to respond to this "normal" behavior?

At this point in our modern-day parenting age, we know that either end of the parenting spectrum is not good for kids: to be strictly authoritarian, insisting on obedience of every command and punishing liberally, sets parents and kids up for more tension and less connection. Being overly permissive as a parent sets up its own set of problems for kids both in and outside the home. So what is the best approach? Well first, try to make sure you are not punishing a child's behavior in response to an unreasonable expectation. Most five- to eight-year-old children should not be expected to sit quietly and calmly at a two-hour long function. Most children this age should not be expected to remember all of the steps of their morning routine without support or occasional reminders. Make sure you are remembering what your child can reasonably handle before punishing them for something they just can't do!

Then, know this: the best way for kids to learn how to adhere to our directives, limits, and expectations is not through punishment, but through practice and praise (Barish 2012). You can think of adherence to directives as a learned skill. While our children are learning and practicing this skill, it is of utmost importance to praise their efforts along the way. This includes praising even when they have ended up acting out or misbehaving.

This may sound like:

→ "I saw how hard you were trying not to lose your cool."
→ "You listened so well when I said it the second time."
→ "You did part of what I asked, how great!"

Especially as it concerns a recurring problem behavior, you want to actively praise when the child refrains from the behavior or shows growth in dealing with their feelings.

Further, we have found through our practice as therapists and as parents that the best, most effective kind of consequence is a natural consequence or a repair. When a child breaks something in a fit of rage, they can spend the afternoon trying to fix the thing they broke, rather than playing outside, or make up the cost through performing household duties that are reasonable for their age. If a child hurts another child physically or emotionally, a repair would be to offer an apology to the child and/or to do something to address the child's hurt or upset feelings, such as draw them a picture, write them a letter, or do a chore on their behalf.

When neither a natural consequence or a repair is available, a brief, easily enforceable punishment can serve an important purpose (Barish 2012). We have a very nuanced view on punishment, so if you are choosing to read this section of the workbook, please read carefully! First things first: again, research has shown that problem child behaviors improve from praise of positive effort and growth and less so from punishment. When children feel connected to their parents and motivated to maintain a positive feeling with them, this is the best, most proactive approach to discipline.

Harsh, excessive punishment rarely teaches a child *anything* about how to sustainably change a problem behavior. What children do learn are ways to avoid punishment, and this can have its own consequences in the form of surreptitious behavior or lying. Frequent punishment also has the power to erode connection and fuel a sense of underlying resentment in kids. They are compliant not because they want to maintain connection, but mostly because they want to avoid getting in trouble (Purvis, Cross, and Sunshine 2007).

Let's be honest: parents sometimes punish when we are at our wit's end and we don't know what else to do. We want to regain a sense of power and control. Our child has broken a rule or refused our directive and we need to show them who's boss. We are not necessarily wrong to think this way: the parent-child hierarchy is extremely important to maintain at this stage of our child's development. If you find yourself doling out harsh punishments in the heat of the moment, those that do not result in improved cooperative behavior, you may want to consider a few go-to consequences of your own that are not as extreme or harsh. A couple of ideas for this may be losing dessert or screen time. If a child is still expecting their normal after-dinner treat, you may say that they can have it only after a serious talk about what happened, so that you can break it down together, as well as come up with a plan to avoid such behaviors in the future. In this case, they have a chance to earn a treat in real time.

For some parents and kids, punishment can be in the form of a look or statement of disapproval that says "This is wrong to do." When you and your child are in a positive, connected place, they will naturally be motivated to get back to a place of peace and connection with you.

REAL-LIFE EXAMPLE

"One of my favorite ways to discipline my children is to call it out, somewhat humorously, as if I am shocked: 'Are you speaking to your mother that way?' 'Are you not listening to your mother?' or I narrate calmly and directly, allowing my child to course correct: 'You are not listening right now.' I may also say something to bring the misbehavior to my child's attention: 'This is the second time I have asked you to get in the shower. What's going on?'"

As in the example above, making a shift to curiosity, a calmly stated "what's happening?" or "what's going on?" when a child disobeys, can be helpful in resolving the problem. When we offer our child the benefit of the doubt (perhaps they didn't hear our directive or are too spent to power through a command), we can support them in collaborating with us and following through on our directives.

For more on the use of collaborative approaches to discipline, see Dr. Ross Greene's Collaborative and Proactive Solutions model.

In studies on Inuit parenting, the style is characterized by a gentle, warm approach, where yelling at small children is considered "demeaning" and there is an active use of playfulness and storytelling to instill discipline and promote respectful behavior in children. Parents model non-reactivity to child misbehavior, staying cool, calm and collected as a model for regulating anger (Doucleff and Greenhalgh 2019).

In sum, our main approach to discipline is to nurture a positive relationship with your child. Fill the well of connection to create a dynamic of cooperation; support appropriate behavior with practice and praise; set age-appropriate limits and expectations; use logical and natural consequences to internalize the impact of negative behaviors; use curiosity to calmly collaborate with your child; make any punishment brief and follow it up with a discussion on how to avoid the problem in the future. The ultimate goal is to get back to a loving place with them.

More Interventions (in Part 2, Discipline Strategies) on Parent and Child Self-Regulation

→ When/Then (page 81)

→ Are You Asking Me for a Compromise? (page 75)

→ Natural & Logical Consequences (page 75)

→ Filling the Well (page 82)

→ Closed-Choice Options (page 78)

→ How to Make a Repair (for Kids) (page 132)

→ Feel Your Escalation (page 60)

→ Pass the Baton (page 69)

CHAPTER 6

WHEN YOU WOBBLE
More on Parent Self-Regulation

This section is devoted to supporting a key component of child self-regulation: parent-self-regulation.

Restating the Basics

A child cannot be expected to learn how to self-regulate if their main caregivers struggle with regulating themselves. Parents have to learn how to become a container for their child's emotional overflow, a lighthouse that gently guides them back to shore, a flagpole staying steady in the flapping of their child's emotion, the bigger, stronger wiser presence for their child. Here, we have our own skill-building to do. It starts with looking more deeply at our history, building our reflective capacities, and gaining support.

The Importance of Our Own History

How we were raised as children impacts the ways we parent (Siegel and Hartzell 2003). This is apparent in myriad ways, from how we uphold traditions and celebrate, to how and what we choose to discipline, to the ways we communicate and connect with our children. Repeating the way we were parented can be both a repetition of the good or bad we felt as kids in our relationship with our parents. We may seek to compensate for what we feel was missing or was harmful to us as children, or the opposite: do our best to re-create it.

REAL-LIFE EXAMPLE

"I remember my mother telling me many times that one thing she didn't want to repeat with us (her daughters) was her mother making her and her brothers sit at the table for a long time even after dinner was over, to finish the plate of food that was served to them. My grandmother grew up with a large family in the depression and always remembered what it was like to not have enough food."

Here is a brief reflective exercise to begin thinking about the ways you were parented:

→ How did your parents express emotion growing up? How did this impact you?

→ How did your parents discipline you? How does that show up in your parenting today?

→ When you were a child, who soothed you in times of stress (times you were sick or upset)? How does that show up in your parenting today?

→ What other aspects of your childhood have impacted your parenting?

You may find yourself wanting to discover more about the links between your past and present. We invite you to explore the many in-depth resources there are on this topic (including *Parenting from the Inside Out,* by Daniel Siegel & Mary Hartzell).

Reflecting on Your Parenting Approaches

You may also look to the future, not just the past, to consider your parenting approaches. Here are three reflective prompts to get you started:

→ What type of adult would you like your child to be someday and what can you do as a parent now to help them get there?

→ How would you like your child to regard you and look back on their childhood when they are an adult?

→ Imagine spending quality time with your adult child. What are your hopes for what this looks and feels like?

Parenting Self: At Your Best and Worst

Good parenting can often go unnoticed, even to ourselves, while "bad" parenting can stick out like a sore thumb, bringing shame and regret. When you consider the times you were functioning at your worst, can you remember all of the times you were on the edge of lashing out, but didn't? All the times you dug deep to push through a challenging moment with your child, keeping your focus on regulating yourself and them? It's likely that the good outweighs the bad. See what it's like to start catching yourself in the "good" moments. How many do you have in a day? Week?

Here are some more reflections from real parents of five- to eight-year-olds:

When you are parenting at your best, what does it look like? How are you feeling in these moments? How is your child feeling?

"I think my best parenting is when I am very rested, happy, and excited to ask them questions, learning more about their lives and talking to them. I feel great during those times, when I get to find out about their lives, and we chat like friends, where I can learn more about how they are with their friends or how they feel about their teachers. Usually the kids are really excited to talk to me about these little private moments they have with their friends. That's the best, that's when I love it the best."

"At my best, I think I am keeping my emotions measured and my communication clear. This goes for the times when I'm being strict or reprimanding as well as those times that I am praising. When I can see my kids understanding why I am making the choices that I am as a parent, it feels great. It feels as though through some stroke of luck, I have discovered the language that we both share."

When you are parenting at your worst, what does it look like? How are you feeling in these moments? How is your child feeling?

"It's usually when I'm frustrated and screaming at them about not doing something that I've been trying to get them to do for a long time, and I'm usually feeling very frustrated and usually tired also. The big thing that I think I always feel is also that nobody is considering *my* feelings, and I think my kids are usually in their own universe and not really even aware of my feelings; they're probably just overwhelmed from hearing me yell."

"At my worst, I am impulsive and emotional. During these times, I'm really only thinking about myself and what needs to be done to make me feel more comfortable and satisfied. I'm usually either angry or frustrated and it unfortunately can manifest in my communication with my kids."

What allows you to be at your best versus your worst as a parent?

"I have to rest usually; I have to get enough rest. When I am not well rested that makes me more short-tempered and more frustrated. Also, I have to set boundaries with them. Everyone's always vying for my attention. I usually have to really quickly set boundaries, like, 'Okay, I can talk to you in a minute, mama has to rest for five seconds.' I have to very calmly set limitations on how much of my time they all require at the same time, and that can be very overwhelming. Usually if I say it with a smile, they are usually respectful of it. But if I don't set boundaries at the beginning, I get attacked from all sides. That's usually what leads to me being overwhelmed and fatigued and talked to from eight different positions. If I can do that I can usually enjoy parenting."

"None of us are perfect, and I think that it's important to recognize that. I think my best is brought out by my desire to relax and listen. When I am fully present with my children, not distracted by work or stress or technology, I feel locked in as a parent. I think stress is the biggest contributor to my parenting fails. If I am distracted by work stressors or marital spats or otherwise feeling unhealthy, it results in worse parenting. I can feel it and I'm sure that my children can as well."

Allow yourself to reflect a bit deeper using these same prompts:

When you are parenting at your best, what does it look like? How are you feeling in these moments? How is your child feeling?

When you are parenting at your worst, what does it look like? How are you feeling in these moments? How is your child feeling?

What allows you to be at your best versus your worst as a parent?

Parents Need Support to Be Well Regulated for Their Kids

As you have likely experienced, there is an important connection between parental self-care and parenting stamina. You are less likely to get frustrated at the normal, everyday annoyances of life after you've had a massage, or relaxed in a hammock on the beach. When you are better able to take care of your adult needs, it's easier for you to be a well-regulated, present parent. Self-care is also a good model for children; if you want your child to become an adult who is able to relax and enjoy life's little pleasures, you can take the time to show them how you do this yourself.

In addition to all the important ways to take care of yourself, we also know "it takes a village to raise a child." Living far from other relatives or lacking sufficient support makes parenting harder! Good parents benefit from having a set of people and resources they can rely on for help. This is especially true for parents of kids with complex emotional or developmental issues and/or parents of kids who have been exposed to early chronic stress or adversity. We can argue that modern-day parenting is harder, more pressure-filled, and more demanding than it ever has been before. A lot of us are no longer living in close-knit communities where support is provided by a network of trusted adults. Nowadays, most of us do not have the help we truly need in order to take best care of ourselves and thrive as parents.

So yes, it takes a village, and wouldn't it be wonderful if this village was made up of people who were always available, offered complimentary skills, and were willing to just jump in and help? If you are parenting with a partner or co-parent, this also applies. Do you and your partner/co-parent have overlapping skills? Families do best when people can step in to perform multiple roles; when you are not the "only one" who can perform an essential function in your family. When one partner or another is too rigid in their capacity to help, it can lead to the other parent's burn-out and resentment. Ideally, you want you and your partner to have great flexibility in your ability to perform essential parenting tasks and share in the mental load.

If you are a single parent, setting boundaries with what you can do as one person alone is an essential parenting skill; it may be even more important to plan ahead and know your limits, being clear with yourself and others on what you can and cannot do. This skill supports you in staying in the zone that is best for you instead of reacting from a place of emotional deficit or overwhelm. It requires monitoring your energy and stress levels, and reflecting on how you feel and why.

Take a moment to consider your village. Who else in your network:

→ Can you trust to watch your kids in case of an emergency?

→ Has a spare set of your house keys?

→ Can pick up or drop off your kids from school or afterschool activities in a pinch?

→ Can give you the evening or weekend off from parenting?

→ Can run an essential errand when needed, like getting medicine or groceries?

→ Can you call if you need to vent and want to feel emotionally supported?

→ Can help you straighten up, cook, or do laundry if you are sick?

Parenting is exponentially harder without a support system. If you are not able to consider many people who can fill these roles, it's important to reflect on how to create this support. Many people are pleased to be asked to step in and help. Consider the trusted adults who care about you and your kids: neighbors, teachers, parents of your child's friends, adult friends. Your network can include services you use or people you hire to help you out. We encourage you to build the network that allows you to better function as a parent.

> **Evolutionary Biology agrees.** Did you know that we are the only species with grandmothers? As Karen Hawkes (Hawkes and Coxworth 2013) explains in her grandmother hypothesis, most female primates do not live past their breeding age. This is different in our species; women can live decades past menopause. These older women can support an ever-growing family line; when new babies are born, they are there to protect and care for the older kids, allowing the parents to continue to focus on procreation while their children can develop in safety. From an evolutionary perspective, this makes natural sense, as the presence of grandmothers allows the family gene to spread.

What trusted elders do you have in your network that may be able to support you and your family?

The Powerful and Positive Effect of Feeling Less Alone

Even if you do not have much of a village, talking with other parents about problems you are having can be so helpful. It has the power to normalize some of the tough moments and experiences we have with our kids. This opening up can help take away the stress, shame, or fears about our parenting woes. A lot of us are afraid to open up to other parents; we worry about being judged. It's important to learn how to how to work with this fear in the service of undoing our aloneness (Fosha 2021).

REAL-LIFE EXAMPLE

"My daughter broke down at a big, end-of-year performance and (almost) could not get on stage. When I opened up and shared this story with another parent, she shared a very similar experience, one where she had invited a small group of family members to her home to watch her child's brief musical performance, only for him to refuse to leave his room and decide at the last minute that he was too nervous! We shared a laugh at the similarities we had with our two very different kids."

Here are the strategies to support your own foundations of Parent self-regulation:

→ Pass the Baton (page 69)

→ All interventions listed in the Parent Self-Regulation section in chapter 8 (page 58)

CHAPTER 7

NOW YOU'VE GOT IT
Staying Steady on the Tightrope

When you feel good about your ability to co-regulate, repair, and fill the well of connection with your child, this section can help you focus on bringing your child's emerging self-regulation skills forward.

How to Build Emotional Resilience in Your Child

As we have discussed, over time and with exposure to many challenging experiences, your child will naturally build resilience in response to upsets. Research has also shown that there are ways to *build* emotional resilience, including the ability to self-regulate (Scientific Council on the Developing Child 2015).

How do we build resilience in children? By allowing them to experience manageable forms of stress, and giving them responsibilities that are a good match for their developing skills. This, in combination with at least one caring, reliable, consistent adult can support further development of emotional resilience.

According to the Harvard Study on the Developing Child (Scientific Council on the Developing Child 2015), there are factors that can be effective in counterbalancing stress, and that generate resilience.

They include being offered opportunities to:

→ Build an internal sense of efficacy

→ Strengthen adaptive skills and the ability to self-regulate

→ Experience a perceived sense of control

We will talk about a few of these factors below.

Building an Internal Sense of Self-Efficacy

Self-efficacy is the internal sense that you can reach your goals, solve problems, and accomplish tasks. When you have high self-efficacy, you believe that you can do well, and that tough tasks are challenges to be mastered, not threats to be avoided (Bandura 1977). High self-efficacy is a supportive force in the face of discouragement, difficulty, or loss. In this way, it serves as a powerful source of self-regulation ("I can do this") in response to challenging or new experiences.

How do we build self-efficacy in our five- to eight-year-old children? This comes through an experience of what psychologists term "mastery"; that is, when you have a sense of personal success and achieve difficult goals. Repeated experiences of mastery help to build confidence in a child as well as the ability to persist through challenges.

Self-efficacy comes from the actual experience kids have of facing a challenge and reaching a goal. Fortunately, at ages five to eight, this sense of mastering something comes in many forms:

→ Tying shoes

→ Learning how to read

→ Scoring a goal at a game

→ Finishing a puzzle, Lego design, or creative endeavor

→ Making a new friend

Positive social models also influence self-efficacy. Learning about kids who can do hard things and accomplish goals, especially kids that your child can relate to, can inspire them to do the same (see Amazing Kids, page 102).

Provide Opportunities to Strengthen Adaptive Skills and the Ability to Self-Regulate

Adaptive skills are those important skills that allow people to function with more and more independence. They go hand in hand with self-regulation because learning to be independent is naturally frustrating; we have to learn to regulate that frustration in order to accomplish our goal of independence.

Adaptive skills help us to adapt to our environments and the expectations placed on us. There are a wide range of adaptive skills, including those required for self-care (bathing, feeding, dressing self), communication (verbal and nonverbal), environment-related (learning how to cross the street safely, how to clean up after oneself), and social (learning how to interact well with others). All kids learn these skills at a different pace (Holbrook 2023).

We can strengthen adaptive skills by allowing children to practice independence. For example, during the busyness of a school week, you may help your child get dressed or tie their shoes in order to get out of the door on time. But at times with less pressure, allow your child to practice these skills independently. The same goes with being automatically responsive to our child's needs. If a child says, "I'm hungry," and starts whining uncontrollably, over time, you may teach them to develop a communication skill that is more adaptive, such as asking them to say, "I'm hungry, what can I have for a snack?" or by coaching them through getting a snack themselves. Kids this age need help with lots of things. However, helping kids too often or too automatically prevents them from growing adaptively and facing the underlying frustration involved with learning a new skill. Here again, feeling the feeling of mild frustration allows a child to learn how to regulate and better cope with it. When they are able to learn a new skill, most kids will delight in this and it will be an opportunity to celebrate their many gains!

Children gain self-esteem when they can feel competent (Erikson 1968). Here are some ways to support adaptive functioning in your child, in the service of their self-regulation skills (Holbrook 2023):

→ Coach your kids through something verbally, without physically helping.

→ Allow more time for a child to complete a challenging task (don't rush them!) and try not to jump in too quickly to help them.

→ Break things down just a bit so they are easier for the child (if you ask them to make a PB & J sandwich, get the items out of the kitchen cupboards for them).

→ Give your child a say in what they may want to do independently.

→ Allow your child to:

- Set the table
- Pick out their clothes
- Feed a pet
- Help with the laundry
- Vacuum
- Wash dishes
- Invent their own forms of play, with no adult help
- Engage in any chore with limited adult supervision

It is important to separate what makes *us* feel good as parents and what makes our kids feel good about themselves. Many parents feel the pressure from those around them to force their children into activities that are popular. It is fun and wonderful to have children try different things, but pay attention to how they respond: If they don't love it, is it because it is hard for them and they just need a little more encouragement, or is it really not a great fit?

REAL-LIFE EXAMPLE

"I remember my eight-year-old daughter gasping and crying across the swimming pool. I had to say, 'You can do it!' many times because learning to swim is an important safety issue for those living near water. When she didn't love soccer, I let her quit!"

Offering a Perceived Sense of Control

A feeling of control is important for anyone, especially children. This is because so much of the child's experience is necessarily controlled and enforced by others. They do not always have the capacity to make decisions that are in their best interest. At times, they have to be controlled as a means to their health and survival. As important as this is, kids also need to feel in control sometimes. This is an important and nourishing feeling, one that is crucial to building resilience.

Not only does a perceived sense of control offer a good feeling, it is also good for kids' brains. When kids have a sense of agency and control, they are better able to use the parts of the brain that help them regulate stress and make good decisions, their developing prefrontal cortex (Stixrud and Johnson 2018).

When kids learn that they can be in control of certain outcomes, it is also a basic way that they can learn to be in in control of themselves (including their own feelings) and have an impact on their immediate environment.

Here are some closed-choice options to offer a child a sense of control or perceived control:

→ "Would you like to sit in the red chair or the blue chair?"

→ "You can choose from any of these healthy snacks."

→ "Once we are at the park you can run as fast as you want to!"

Tying It All Together

Parenting can feel like walking a tightrope, requiring balance and flexibility, structure and practice, and focus on the present with an eye toward the future. We need to be attuned to ourselves and to our child in order to co-regulate. We need to offer a ton of co-regulation for a child to begin to learn to self-regulate. We need to create a well of connection and delight in our child in order to support their sense of unconditional lovability (a baseline for self-regulation). We need to set appropriate limits and repair when we make inevitable errors. We need to hold compassion and grace for ourselves and our kids in order to maintain our stamina as parents and connection with our kids. We need to give kids an experience of control and independence, allowing them to experience the mild stress that supports their adaptive skills. We need to use our imagination and bravery, and model our own self-regulation skills. We need a village to nourish and support us in doing this hard work. Read ahead for the many ways we have discussed applying these concepts in the real world.

PART 2
STRATEGIES

Use this section to enhance the concepts discussed in the previous section and/or as a quick reference. Many of these strategies are time-tested and research-based, and others have been generated from the trial and error of our own parenting, and that of the many parents and families we have worked with. Please be sure to tailor these strategies for your own individual needs.

CHAPTER 8

STRATEGIES FOR PARENT SELF-REGULATION
What to Do for YOU

HOW TO APPLY IMAGINATION, COURAGE, AND HONESTY

Intervention 1: Imagination. Find a photograph of yourself at the same age as your child is now. Think about yourself at that time. What was life like for you? Use this reflection to help you imagine your own child's life. Write about it here:

_____

_____

_____

_____

Intervention 2: Courage. Think about a parent or teacher or even a character from a TV show, movie or book that you know and admire. How would this person parent in a way that is different from what you are doing now? How would they use courage in their parenting? Write about it here:

_____

_____

_____

_____

Intervention 3: Honesty. Write a note to your pre-parent self. Share your honest feelings about this stage of parenting. What would you say about all of the good, the bad and the crazy-making of parenting a 5- to 8-year-old?

_____

_____

_____

_____

_____

PLAYING WITH ATTUNEMENT

We can learn a lot about the felt experience of attunement from music, specifically from call-and-response songs. These songs mimic human communication and the practice of being in sync with one another. One set of lyrics catches the other, and a pattern is formed. The ubiquity of these kinds of songs, first shared in the Americas by enslaved West Africans, is present in cultures around the world and across musical genres. When music is used in the military, at sports games, in religious ceremonies, and as work songs, you can be reminded that you do not have to face hard, mundane, repetitive, or intimidating life experiences all on your own. Just as importantly, songs can simply be a fun, full-bodied way to connect in the present with others.

Here are some favorites:

→ "Shout," The Isley Brothers, 1959

→ "We Will Rock You," Queen, 1977

→ "Banana Boat (Day-O)," Harry Belafonte, 1955

→ "ABC," The Jackson 5, 1970

→ "Let's Call the Whole Thing Off," Ella Fitzgerald and Louis Armstrong, 1957

→ "California Dreamin'," The Mamas and the Papas, 1965

→ "Did you Feed my Cow?," Ella Jenkins, 1966

→ "Águas De Março," Elis Regina, Antonio Carlos Jobim, 1974

→ "Wanna Be Startin' Somethin'," Michael Jackson, 1982

→ "Can I Kick It?," A Tribe Called Quest, 1990

- → "Dueling Banjos," Arthur "Guitar Boogie" Smith, 1955
- → "Victor Vito," Laurie Berkner, 1999
- → "Do Wah Diddy Diddy," Manfred Mann version, 1964
- → "Ché Ché Colé," Willie Colón, Héctor Lavoe, 1972

Play a song together with your child to get a different feel for attunement, as well as for a fun, connecting experience.

FEEL YOUR ESCALATION

When our children have a tantrum, ignore us, or disobey us it can activate deep feelings. The key is catching this wave of intense emotion (anger, frustration, or helplessness), and to trust that the best and desired outcome is to remain calm. Here is a strategy you may use to help:

Imagine building a wall around yourself, brick by brick. At first, it's low enough for you to simply step over the bricks to the other side. As you build a little higher, you can still step up and over, but with a little more effort. As you get up to your waist, there is still time, technically, to get out. Once you are up to your shoulders in bricks, it's a bit too late to step over them. In this case, you have to make a hole through one of the sides and come back to repair it later.

Each brick stands for the physical, mental, and emotional cues you have for emotional escalation with your child. In our minds and bodies, these bricks may sound, feel, and look like:

- → "My child is ignoring me."
- → "I am feeling disrespected."
- → Feeling "heated"
- → Thinking negative thoughts toward your child
- → Thinking negative thoughts toward yourself
- → Getting angry at something small that you normally wouldn't
- → "How many times do I have to say it?"
- → Shaking your head

- → "This is embarrassing."
- → "I would have never done this/said this when I was a child."
- → Face flushing
- → Chest tightening
- → Jaw clenching
- → Blood pressure rising
- → Starting to raise voice
- → "When will this stop?"
- → "I am too tired for this."

Make a list of your own bricks here:

1. _____

2. _____

3. _____

Whatever kind of bricks you have, practice counting your bricks. No, we cannot keep track of every trigger at every moment. However, keep an eye on how high that wall is getting for you, and see if you can still step over it. There are lots of options on the other side of the wall.

When you feel that you're escalating, one of the best strategies in these moments is to do *nothing*. Interacting with your child during these moments is likely to add fuel to the fire. When you are heated, doing nothing in the moment can have many more benefits than drawbacks.

Another option: Take some time to regroup. If you can, let your child know you need a moment to calm yourself and that you will be back (see more on how to de-escalate your intense emotions on page 62).

Swap out. If another calm adult is present, see if you can trade places for a moment, letting that adult know you need some time to regulate (see Pass the Baton strategy, page 69).

Important: Remember that if you are too heated to engage with your child, you can always come back to the situation later! You can talk it over with your child that afternoon or the next day. You can say, "Remember yesterday when we had to go to the grocery store and you got so upset? I was frustrated too. Let's talk about what happened."

REAL-LIFE EXAMPLE

"We had just left a family member's birthday party. My seven-year-old daughter, who has recently been in a 'no cake' phase, decided to skip the birthday cake. Afterwards, when talking about the party, I mentioned how this cake was an interesting one. It was a cookie cake, not a traditional birthday cake. Upon hearing this, my daughter stopped in her tracks and started jumping up and down, angry and disappointed that she had not realized her grave oversight. She was mad at everyone—the birthday girl who didn't tell her, her mom who didn't make sure she knew, the other kids and parents who were eating away. With each jump and stomp to the ground, I could feel my escalation. How could she act so ungratefully? It's not my fault that she didn't realize what kind of cake it was! How dare she act like this in public! She is embarrassing me!"

Here, with all of these emotions and thoughts piled up, a parent's best option may be to do nothing. You may remain present for your child while keeping some focus on regulating yourself. With your non-response as a regulation source for yourself and your child, your child can eventually calm down. Once your own brain is able to come back online, you can think a bit more clearly.

BACK TO THIS PARENT'S REAL-LIFE EXAMPLE

"I decided to remain as calm as possible, continue walking home, and address the behavior another time. Patting her on the back, we then continued on walking. At home, we talked about the upsetting episode. I reminded her of all the ways she has handled feelings of disappointment and frustration in the past. I also joked that the cookie cake was pretty dry and flavorless, and that she didn't miss anything! Looking back on it, my daughter agreed that she had a big reaction to a small thing. With this perspective in her mind, I hoped that she may be more equipped to deal with small disappointments in the future."

HOW TO DE-ESCALATE: OPTIONS TO DISMANTLE THE BRICKS

Coaching yourself through a heated moment with your child is a good way to de-escalate yourself and maintain your goal of remaining calm.

Here are some phrases to use during these moments:

→ My child is having a hard time; it's temporary.

→ My only goal is to remain calm.

→ I can get through this.

→ My child's tantrum will pass as I remain calm.

→ My child and I will ride out this tough moment.

→ Doing nothing right now is my best option.

→ My anger in this moment is not worth harming the relationship with my child.

Add your own to this list:

_____

_____

_____

_____

Here are some behavioral and sensory regulation techniques to use when you are escalated:

→ If your child is safe, leave the area and go to another room for a few minutes. You can say, "I'll be right back," or, "I just need a minute."

→ Stick your head in the freezer, splash your face with cold water, chew on some ice, or drink some ice water.

→ Look out of a window or focus on an image.

→ Put on your headphones and listen to music or a podcast for a few minutes (do not ignore your child completely if they are still upset).

→ Focus on your breathing.

→ Smell something that calms you, like a special soap, lotion, candle, or perfume.

Add your own to this list:

_____

_____

_____

_____

In sum: feeling and monitoring your escalation are the keys to remaining calm. Try to keep track of how many bricks are building up around you. When you are too heated to engage with your child, do nothing. You can also walk away for a few minutes. Try swapping out with a calm adult if available, or use a de-escalation strategy.

MOVE THE GOAL POST

This is an intervention featuring flexibility as the key component to parent emotional regulation. Use flexibility to solve or reduce the impact of a problem and model this as a coping skill for your children.

Sometimes the goal, the way you want something to happen, can be the problem itself. If you change the goal by moving the goal post, you can reduce stress.

Example: It's a morning with a lot of unexpected obstacles, you are frustrated, stressed, and you still want to get your child to school on time.

Move the goal post: You strive to be at school within five minutes of opening and tell yourself, life happens!

Example: A friend calls with upsetting news. You no longer have the time or energy to make dinner.

Move the goal post: You serve breakfast for dinner.

Add your own example here:

Example:

_____

_____

Move the goal post:

_____

_____

INCREASING EMPATHY

What are your instincts when:

→ Your child wakes up from a bad dream and runs into your room?

→ Your child has an accident and hurts him/herself?

→ Your child's feelings are hurt by a friend?

What are your instincts when:

→ Your child is throwing a tantrum?

→ Your child is hungry or tired and is whining?

→ Your child throws something, hits, or slams a door in anger?

How do these instincts compare? You may notice that your instincts to the first set of behaviors are to soothe and comfort your child, while the instincts in the second set are to control, limit, or punish their behavior.

Imagine for a moment what it may be like to respond to your child's vulnerable states, such as waking up from a bad dream, with control, limits, or punishment. How painful to imagine! Good parents work to summon the best version of themselves at these moments, even when it is hard.

Now, what is it like to imagine using these instincts to soothe and comfort in response to a different kind of vulnerability, like when our children are overcome with emotions such as anger, jealousy, or sadness?

As a practice in empathy building, take a few minutes to imagine this. How does it feel to you to respond to your child's anger the way you would if they got hurt? Does a combination of both these soothing and comforting behaviors along with limits feel like the right fit at moments like these?

Note your reflections here:

HINDSIGHT IS 20/20

This is a strategy meant to help you avoid and mitigate stress.

When your child is predictably having a challenge to the same circumstance, they may need an accommodation of some kind. For example, if you know your child always needs to use the bathroom before leaving their after-school program, you bring them to the bathroom, even when they say they don't have to (you've been there before, left trying to find a bathroom with a child who all the sudden "can't hold it").

Here are some other common "live and learn" moments in five- to eight-year-olds, and how you can plan ahead:

→ Child has a hard time sharing a certain toy. *Make it unavailable during a play date.*

→ Child always asks to go into a toy store that you pass, and you do not have time to go in. *Go a different route to avoid passing it.*

→ You know it will rain tomorrow, and the child's outdoor plans will be canceled. *Plan a fun alternative.*

→ Child is predictably hungry, full of energy, cold, or grumpy after school (or after some other activity). *Have a solution and your own mood ready to deal with this.*

Some of you might be saying to yourselves: I will just make my child wear an extra layer or my child is spoiled if they insist on looking in the toy store. As discussed earlier, with a still-developing brain, children don't have the capacity to plan ahead or regulate their emotions easily, so many times it is most effective (and pleasant!) for us to use our adult brains and avoid predictable problems.

What are some plan-ahead moments you can consider for your child?

_____

_____

_____

_____

_____

What is your solution to resolve or avoid the predictably challenging situation?

_____

_____

_____

_____

_____

> Of special note, if your child has repeated meltdowns under certain conditions or acts out in some way, they may not be quite ready for that experience and should instead work toward it in smaller steps.

ZOOM OUT

Zooming Out from the moment and reflecting on your child holistically can be one of the most important and loving acts of parenting. Zooming Out is a form of mentalizing. It is when we put our child's acting-out behavior in context, remembering that it may be a culmination of many upsets, strained, or hurt feelings they have carried throughout their day (see Story about Disappointment, from 8 to 81 Years Old on page 36). When Zooming Out, consider the impact of environmental and relational shifts in the child's life, including at home, school, the greater community, and their physical environment. You can consider your own stress level or things you may be going through as a parent as part of this greater context. This also is a supportive way to keep empathy available for our children and ourselves.

REAL-LIFE EXAMPLE

"When my son was five, he suddenly began having a harder time with routines and limits at home and school, and was more easily frustrated and more irritable than normal. In considering what may have been impacting him, I thought about all of the variables and changes in his life: it was approaching the end of his last year in preschool, and everyone around him was talking about this transition. His little sister, whom he adored, had just been born two months earlier. He was also having a hard time adjusting to daylight savings time and wasn't getting as much sleep as he was used to. By taking all of these things into account, I was able to realize that his little body and brain were carrying a whole lot of feelings and discomforts. From this place, I could engage him with more connection, patience, and empathy, which was the gentle shift he needed in me to feel back to himself!"

REAL-LIFE EXAMPLE

"I often found that when my five- to eight-year-old kids were dysregulated, the next day they were obviously ill. It took me many years of parenting to finally remember to ask if they were feeling okay!"

You can also Zoom Out for yourself. If you haven't been parenting at your best, it may help to put this in the context of other stressors you are experiencing. Have these stressors been making you more tired and have less patience? This way you can have more empathy for yourself and see if you can make adjustments to the stressors that are impacting your parenting stamina.

Take a moment to reflect on a tough phase or recurring issue you are having with your child. Describe it here:

_____

_____

_____

_____

_____

Zoom out to explore what external stressors and changes could be connected to this problem:

_____

_____

_____

_____

PLANNED IGNORING

This strategy is for when you have no gas in your tank and feel on the edge of escalation. Take note that this strategy is not strictly for the purpose of ignoring a child's attention-seeking behavior. Instead, this is for the ADULT to use for the purposes of self-regulation. When you plan to ignore an irksome or nagging behavior from your child, you can save yourself some aggravation. You can tell yourself, "I am choosing to ignore this." Stay present but ignore.

Here are all of the things you can choose to ignore for your own sense of regulation and control:

→ When your child is whining and frustrated asking for food, in the moments just before you are about to serve them.

→ When you have already said "no" (in some way) to your child's request and they keep asking you.

→ When your child has an overreaction to a typical transition or limit that they have adhered to many times.

→ Please add your own example here: _____

Things **not** to ignore:

→ Anything aggressive or harmful to your child or others

→ When your child deliberately defies your boundary (e.g., takes your phone from your bag and starts using it when you have said "no")

→ Any inappropriate or dangerous behavior in the car. Pull over as soon as you can to deal with it.

PASS THE BATON

Pass the Baton is a strategy for use with a partner. It can be used in two ways: either in a stressful moment or in response to a routinely stressful part of the day or week:

1. In a stressful moment, it can be helpful to have a code word for one partner to signal "distress" and the other to take over. For example, if somehow all of the children are clinging on you while your partner walks ahead, watches TV in the other room, or is on their phone in the very same room, you might say, "Aren't you lonely all by yourself?!" A family with a firefighter dad used the code word "blanket," which meant he was about to lose his cool. It was short for "wet blanket" to quell a fire, and when said, the mom knew that it was time to intervene and pitch in. Many parents say that they have to use the bathroom and then text their partner to say that they need some help!

2. When reflecting on times that are routinely stressful, it is good for you and your partner to think about whether the right person is handling the job. Are you especially stressed by the morning or bedtime routine? Is the person who has an early morning team meeting taking the kids to school? Probably not a good idea unless your kids love early-bird drop-off! Can one person get up with a sick or scared kid in the night and the other get up with kids first in the morning? Does one parent not mind going to all the sports games, and the other, all of the art classes?

One very important thing to note: figuring out how to amicably share care for your children is a private adult conversation.

IS THIS A DEVELOPING SKILL??

When our kids become dysregulated, it may be for many different reasons. When searching for what is underneath the behavior, consider that they are still developing. Even when a skill has been developed, a child may not have it down consistently.

Here are some skills five- to eight-year-olds are still developing. Circle the ones your child is working on right now:

→ Adjusting to new situations and new people

→ Keeping track of personal belongings

→ Expressing feelings and concerns with words

→ Managing frustration and persisting with difficulty

→ Accepting limits

→ Dealing with transitions

→ Getting ready independently

→ Cleaning up after themselves

→ Managing boredom

→ Understanding the impact of their behavior on others/perspective taking

→ Modulating their voice

→ Controlling impulses

→ Self-monitoring (being able to tell how big emotions are becoming)

→ Other developing skill: _____

→ Other developing skill: _____

→ Other developing skill: _____

Parent strategy: Leave yourself a reminder. In a place you will often see it, post a sticky note that says, "I have a child still working on X." See what it's like to keep this in mind, as a tool to develop compassion for your growing child and the very many complicated things they have to learn.

Child strategy: See Practice Makes Progress (page 77) and Try Again (page 79) for more support on building skills your child is still developing.

CHAPTER 9

DISCIPLINE STRATEGIES THAT SUPPORT PARENT AND CHILD SELF-REGULATION
What to Do for You and Your Child

USING DIRECTIVES PLAYFULLY

When issuing a directive, see what it's like to change your style: approach your child and whisper what you would like to have them do (instead of yelling it from across the room), say it in an accent, sing it, or say it in a funny voice. Come up with your own playful alternative and see what it's like. How does it work for you?

REAL-LIFE EXAMPLES

"One of my favorites was to sing my thoughts to my kids. Even in my not-so-great opera voice!"

"When I give my kids a directive, I often end with a playful, yet firm, 'You got me?' to ensure my child has heard me and understood my directive."

Attempt A: Give directive from across the room.

Attempt B: Whisper, sing, or speak directive in a funny voice.

There's always...

Attempt C: Give directive with a physical prompt (hand on child's shoulder), eye contact, and at their level.

How did these compare?

Another option for this is using child-friendly symbols and characters:

→ Please be quiet for a few minutes, like a mouse.

→ Get your shoes on, super fast, like a magician!

→ Stand calmly, like a statue!

USE OF PRAISE AND CONNECTED PRAISE

As we discussed, the best way for kids to learn how to adhere to our directives, limits, and expectations is through practice and praise. Praising your child is also important for developing your child's positive view of themselves and as a form of connection between you and your child. We believe in praising effort more than outcome, and things little, teeny, and big. As long as it is coming from an authentic place, praise liberally! Here are some examples of language you can use:

→ I see you trying so hard!

→ I can tell you are really focusing!

→ I love the colors you chose.

→ It's easy to see how brave you are.

→ I noticed how kind you were to your sibling.

→ I noticed the way you waited and asked first.

→ Add your own: _____

→ Add your own: _____

In relation to praising effort, it is also a lovely option to praise your child's unique self and the way they make you feel. This is praise that is connected to the relationship, or, "connected praise."

Here are some examples of connected praise:

→ Seeing you try again makes me so proud.

→ You can really make me laugh.

→ I like the way you are waiting quietly.

→ I love spending time with you.

→ You are such a helpful child.

→ You have really interesting ideas.

→ I am so glad I know someone like you!

→ I love being your mom/dad/papa/mama/grandma/grandpa.

→ Add your own: _____

→ Add your own: _____

See the very sweet "Proud Song" (Sesame Street, 2012) between Elmo and his Dad, Louie.

Allow your child to "overhear" you praising them. Speak on the phone or with another adult within earshot of your child, share something you are proud your child did, including the details. Example: "I saw him working so hard on his drawing, I could tell he was getting frustrated, but he kept with it. He is so determined. His drawing was so well-done, wait until you see it!"

USE OF CONNECTED REWARDS

These kinds of rewards center the relationship between the caregiver and the child.. This is a form of "feeding the well" of parent-child regulation. Having enough water in the well is also intrinsic to child self-regulation; it allows children to be more emotionally flexible. Having fun with your child keeps your relationship strong for those times when you are not feeling well physically and emotionally or don't respond to them as your best self.

When you feel compelled to reward your child for their hard work, reaching a milestone, or other reasons, it is tempting to give them the things they may beg for or want (e.g., games, toys, candy, etc.).

Although it's always okay to offer those things some of the time, other times, in the service of child-parent connection, these relationship-centered rewards can work beautifully:

→ Allow your child to make an adult decision, such as choosing the dinner, dessert, or a family activity at home for the night.

→ Allow your child dress up time in your clothes, shoes, or jewelry.

→ Make a cake, cookies, or brownies together.

→ Allow your child to choose a family outing.

→ Have a "yes" hour (within reason) at home.

Make a list here of connected rewards that would work well in your family:

1. _____

2. _____

3. _____

> Sometimes it is fun to have a reward that the whole family can work toward. For example, "If we can all get out the door together on time this week, let's have a pizza night on Friday." Can you think of one connected reward that would work for your whole family?

OFFERING ALTERNATIVES AND EXPLAINING WHY

When giving a directive such as "get off the couch" or "stop playing" you have some tools that may support your child's responsiveness to these directives.

You can offer an alternative to the behavior with direct communication:

→ You can draw on this paper (instead of the floor).

→ Use walking feet in the house (instead of running).

→ You can speak quietly (instead of so loudly!).

→ Add your own here: _____

The aim is to give or teach the alternative, *not* just to correct. That way, your child can know what to do, not just what not to do.

You can explain why:

"Stop playing in five minutes" versus "It's time to stop playing because we are leaving the house very soon to meet grandma, and we don't want to annoy her by being late."

"Sit at the table" versus "I am worried your drink is going to spill on the carpet. Let's have you sit at the table."

"Change your dress shirt for playing" versus "I don't want your special shirt to get dirty or ripped. Let's put it back on the hanger and you can pick another shirt to play in."

ARE YOU ASKING ME FOR A COMPROMISE?

In her wonderful book (with David Cross and Wendy Lyons Sunshine) *The Connected Child*, Karyn Purvis has some great parenting ideas. As you may have guessed from the title, the book, much as we do here in this workbook, focuses on the balance between "connecting and correcting." When your child is ignoring you or misbehaving, it can be very effective to ask them if they would like a compromise. Just as in the example from "Planned Ignoring," if your child is begging for food while you are almost ready to serve dinner, you could ask, "Would you like a compromise?" And then the child could ask if they could have a tiny snack to hold them over while you are getting the rest of the dinner on the table. And then you can say, "Sure!"

"Are you asking me for a compromise?" Is one of my favorite strategies to use when a child has ignored my directive. It almost always generates a cooperative response in my child, and once they are engaged we can move forward. For example:

Parent: "It's time for bed!"

Child: No response/Ignores me.

Parent: "Are you asking me for a compromise?"

Child: "Yes, may I have 10 more minutes?"

Parent: "You can have five."

Child: "Okay."

Parent: "So what did we agree on?"

Child: "Five more minutes before bed."

Tip: Before using this technique, introduce the concept of "compromise" to your child. You might say, "a compromise is when people work together to find a solution."

NATURAL AND LOGICAL CONSEQUENCES

Life is full of natural and logical consequences. If you are late for the flight, you will miss the plane; if you break or lose something important, you may have to pay to replace it or learn to live without it. When we can't fix a problem, we have to accept the consequences, and this can be very disappointing or frustrating. We can also learn from these experiences, both in managing our own feelings as well as planning ahead or being more cautious.

When our children are very small, the vast majority of the time, we are protecting them from the world around them. It is a slow process to pull back and let them experience the consequences of their own actions as they grow older.

At ages five to eight, when they are developmentally more able to handle life's natural consequences, overshielding children can impede emotional development and maturity. Learning how to handle negative emotions, with the support of a compassionate parent, is a cornerstone of emotional regulation.

Examples of logical consequences:

→ Child breaks favorite toy; toy no longer available
→ Child drops their ice cream cone; no more ice cream (however, you can be very sympathetic and offer to share your own)
→ Not ready for school; late for class
→ Messy room; can't find things that they might need/have to cancel playdate
→ Not doing homework; consequence happens at school

Below are some example scenarios with possible options.

Example: Your child is touching a cat in a way the cat does not like.

Options:

1. You move the cat into another room and shut the door.
2. You tell your child not to touch the cat multiple times, but they continue.
3. You do nothing and the cat hisses and bats at your child.

Example: Your child leaves their library book outside in the backyard.

Options:

1. You bring the book in yourself.
2. You tell your child many times that they need to bring in the book.
3. You do nothing and the book gets rained on.

In the examples above, it might be appropriate to give one warning or reminder, but in the long run, you will have the best outcomes if you choose option 3 in both examples. Your child will learn nothing from options 1 and 2.

It is also okay to be sympathetic after something negative happens. You might give hem a hug if they are crying. Or you might say, "Oh no, I guess the cat didn't like that. Are you okay?" or

"Oh boy, let's talk to the librarian and see what it costs to replace it. Maybe you can do a job for Grandma to earn some money to pay for it. Or maybe you will have some ideas."

This kind of parenting is really important. It is good parenting to allow children to experience the mild to moderate consequences of their actions.

If you have a hard time with this type of parenting, it will be helpful to ask yourself: What am I afraid of? What is the worst thing that can happen? Am I doing this for myself or for my child?

REAL-LIFE EXAMPLE

"My mother once told me that she had drunk a jar of pickle juice against her mother's advice, which then made her sick. She never did it again—and neither did I try it! My grandmother didn't lock away the pickles knowing that it wasn't dangerous to drink the juice but rather let my mother experience the harmless but unpleasant consequences."

For more on this topic see: *Parenting with Love & Logic* (2020) by Foster Cline & Jim Fay.

PRACTICE MAKES PROGRESS: THE IMPORTANCE OF PRACTICING A SKILL

Mastery of any skill requires persistence, repetition, and experiential practice. We all learn important skills through practice. This is the same for kids learning how to deal with intense emotions such as frustration and disappointment. It's much harder for kids to learn the skills and behaviors we expect through lecturing or punishment. A better option is praising the efforts they make along the way.

Note one thing here that you would like your child to make progress with:

Example: A 7-year-old is still working on managing disappointment and frustration using words, not actions (jumping up and down, falling to floor, screaming, throwing).

What are the steps they need to take?

Example: Practice use of go-to phrases for mild frustration (Aww man! That's frustrating!).

_____

_____

What will success look like?

Example: Expressing frustration with mostly words.

_____

_____

How will you notice the efforts they are making along the way?

Example: Offering praise every time child can express frustration or disappointment with words.

_____

_____

How long do you think it will take them to improve?

_____

Tip: If your child gets dysregulated frequently, have "fire drills." Instead of stop, drop, and roll, you can ask them to practice having a fit and then going to a carpet, the couch, or their bed and staying there until they are calm. Switch locations so they can pretend to melt down and then go to the calm place.

→ Where is a good place for your child to calm down?

→ What can you call this drill?

→ When will you practice? How often should you do this? Weekly? Daily?

→ Did you remember to praise them?

CLOSED-CHOICE OPTIONS

This is a great option for strong-willed kids who want or need to feel a semblance of control. As we discussed in the section, Offering a Perceived Sense of Control (page 54), the parent sets the parameters, but the child gets to work within those parameters to make a choice.

→ Would you like to put on your brown shoes or black shoes?

→ Would you like to get in the shower now or in five minutes?

You can also use a closed-choice option to reduce conflict or diffuse power struggles between you and your child. Here is an example of how it can be used for high emotion moments or problem behaviors:

Keep the choice in the child's hands rather than as a battle between you. The essence of this approach is "it's up to you," with as little parental influence as possible.

Example:

→ You can choose to put away your toys or leave them on the floor and only play with them again when you can show me that you can clean up. It's up to you.

→ You can choose to continue running and being loud and we leave the library or we can read a book and sit quietly for a while. It's up to you.

Try this approach as an experiment. Use it when your child typically digs in their heels and seeks control. What happens when you give your child a sense of power, one that is completely designed by your own boundaries? You may notice this takes more effort; it's a shift in mindset and approach.

Write a little about the outcome of your experience here:

TRY AGAIN

This is a great strategy to use when helping your child practice tone or delivery in their responses or requests. This helps them remember that it is not just *what* you say, but *how* you say something that matters. In the moment that a child responds to you in an inappropriate way, you can ask them to "try again." If your child is working on asking for things or making statements with a tone of calm or kindness, practicing this may give support. A lot of kids this age have no intention of being rude or inappropriate with their tone; many are still learning how to modulate their voice, use manners, and/or express themselves effectively.

Example: It's close to bedtime and you asked your child to get in the shower. She shouts:

> **Child:** But we haven't had dessert yet!!!

> **Mom:** (Calm, pausing with eye contact.) Let's try that again.

> **Child:** Can we please have our ice cream before the shower?

> **Mom:** Sure thing.

How would you respond to these demands below?

Get my jacket!

_____

_____

_____

_____

I want a cookie!

_____

_____

_____

_____

Give me the iPad!

_____

_____

_____

_____

ALL OF THE WONDERFUL WAYS TO SAY "NO"

If you have found yourself struggling with setting a firm limit, here are some options to play with, other than simply saying "no:"

→ Not at this time.

→ Unfortunately, no.

→ Not right now.

→ I cannot at the moment.

→ The clock says it is time for bed/to go/etc.

→ I wish I could!

→ That is enough for tonight.

→ I would if I could.

→ Yes, definitely, as soon as you...

→ Yes, we can tomorrow!

→ Picking up your child's stuffed animal and saying in a funny voice, "It is so annoying when your mom says, "No!"

Circle the ways that you have tried above and underline the ones that have worked best.

> It's best to explore more about why saying "no" may be hard. Setting firm limits with warmth is a key component to child self-regulation, as it helps kids practice dealing with frustration.

WHEN/THEN

Using the conjoining words "When... then..." is a straightforward way to set an expectation and agree to your child's desired outcome, all without having to give a straightforward command (one that can often trigger a shutdown response from your child). Here is an example of this exchange between parent and child:

Child: Can I go outside and play?

Parent: When you clean up your toys, then you can go outside.

Child: Can I have dessert?

Parent: When you put your plate in the sink, then I can give you dessert.

Child: I want the red Popsicle!

Parent: When you ask with your manners, then you can have the color you want.

Child: I don't want to go to bed!

Parent: When you tell me you are ready for bedtime and a story, then I can read to you in your comfy bed.

FILLING THE WELL

Filling the well of connection between parent and child is our main discipline strategy. As we stated earlier, a positive well of connection allows children to make better use of their own brains, as well as your support in managing and recovering from upsets. Connection feeds a child's inner sense of goodness and lovability; through this connection they can more easily recover from upsets and return to a state of calm.

In addition to playing together (see 5 to 15 minutes of playing ideas on page 24), what are some activities that have a high rate of success for engaging and bonding with your child? See if you can increase the water in your well. Perhaps you can be intentional about adding in such activities at least once a week, if you can.

Here are some examples:

→ Baking a cake

→ Having an indoor or outdoor picnic

→ Dancing

→ Going somewhere new and exciting

→ Exploring nature

→ Looking at baby pictures and old movies together

→ Watching your child's favorite cartoon or movie with them, giving it your full attention

→ Playing together with a pet

→ Visiting a favorite place

→ Playing sports together

→ Making art together

The list can go on and on… add your own ideas here:

_____

_____

_____

_____

_____

_____

_____

_____

CHAPTER 10

STRATEGIES TO SUPPORT CHILD SELF-REGULATION

We can help our babies calm down by picking them up; while this may still be helpful for some five- to eight-year-olds, it is important to work on supporting their own self-regulation. Here we include a range of strategies to support your child, including use of co-regulation, ways to soothe their upsets physically, through use of validation, and other strategies. The idea is that over time, your child will learn these approaches in order to help themselves.

Physical Regulation as a Baseline Approach

Movement and physical sensation are some of our earliest tools for soothing distress. We swaddle and rock a baby to soothe them, give a toddler a warm bath to settle them down, or use soft lighting and music to help a little one gently fall off to sleep. These interventions can soothe an upset nervous system in ways that words cannot. It's also important to remember that for young kids, vigorous daily movement is an essential part of their ability to feel regulated, release tension, and discharge excess energy. Knowing what sensory and physical aids best soothe your child is a key regulation strategy!

> Movement can help with regulating many emotions. It's a way of practicing "integration" (Siegel and Bryson 2012), or aligning the *emotionally-driven* parts of the brain with the more evolved *cognitive* parts of the brain. Movement has the potential to calm the parts of the brain that become activated during times of stress or upsetting experiences.

When a child's nervous system is activated and they are acting out or melting down, something that is meant to soothe and regulate the body can be incredibly helpful. After providing initial soothing (getting down to your child's level, staying regulated, using as soothing and calming of a voice as possible, being as warm as you can), you can invite them to do something physical.

Alternatively, for some kids, initial soothing won't be helpful and you can offer the following directly or after a few moments of calm silence:

→ Chew on some carrots.

→ Drink some warm tea.

→ Take a hot bath.

→ Have a bear hug.

→ Wheelbarrow.

→ Get wrapped in a tight blanket.

→ Hold some ice in your hands.

→ Put an ice pack on your face.

If your child is so dysregulated that you can't use any words, try giving them a piece of gum, walking outside, or tossing a ball. Then, connect with your words when they are calm.

> Feeling the "container" of our bodies can help us realize that even when we have a big emotion, we remain intact; when we are able to move, breathe, and feel our heartbeats, it's a simple reminder that perhaps everything will eventually be okay. Along these lines, you might say to your child, "Let me feel your heartbeat" with "Oh my! Your heart is beating fast! Should we try some breathing together and see if we can calm it down?"

For more on calming strategies using sensory regulation approaches, see the very helpful *Understanding your Child's Sensory Signals* by Angie Voss.

CALM BODIES

Flexibility is a big component of being able to stay emotionally regulated. This includes learning how to shift from an energetic state to a calmer one. It can help kids to learn to self-regulate by continually practicing this shift. Kids with a ton of energy or who have been going through a stormy period with big emotions would benefit from extra doses of calming their bodies.

There are so many good options for calming the body. Experiment with the following ideas to get an idea of what works for your child:

- → Calming music
- → White noise or nature sounds at bedtime or quiet times
- → Weighted blanket for relaxation or sleep
- → Patting the back
- → Foot massage
- → Calming scents for the bath, in a diffuser or as a lotion
- → Listening to a story via audiobook or parent reading to them
- → Bath/shower time with calming scents

- → Using a meditation app such as Headspace for children ages five to eight
- → Taking a calm walk outside on a pleasant evening
- → Slow down pace of day/amount of activities
- → Turn off screens for all in the household
- → Quiet down the house
- → Dim the lights
- → Calm yourself
- → Use breathing techniques (page 129)

List your own ideas here:

_____   _____

_____   _____

_____   _____

_____   _____

USE OF VALIDATION FOR CHILD'S EMOTIONAL EXPRESSIONS[1]

Validation is when you listen hard and acknowledge another person's truth. It's a powerful co-regulation tool.

Invalidation is when you do not acknowledge another person's perspective or downplay their feelings (e.g., saying "What's the big deal?" or " Why are you crying about one little thing?").

---

1 Exercises in this section based on: National Alliance on Mental Illness. "Validating & Invalidating Statements and Curious Questions." https://namibrevard.org/Information/Validating-and-Invalidating-Statements.pdf.

Before reading ahead, think of examples of when you have been validating and invalidating to your child and write them down here:

Validating:

_____

_____

_____

Invalidating:

_____

_____

_____

Imagine talking to a friend about a tough time you are going through. What would feel like a more helpful response from them?

Script A

> **You:** I am going through a stressful time.
>
> **Friend:** I hate it when that happens to me.
>
> **You:** It's been really hard to deal with.
>
> **Friend:** Well, life's not fair.
>
> **You:** I wish I had more support.
>
> **Friend:** You always get yourself into these situations.

What is your reaction to how this friend is responding? How did you feel reading these responses? Imagine that feeling in your child's body, keeping in mind their developing ability to regulate strong emotions.

Script B

> **You:** I am going through a stressful time.
>
> **Friend:** What a tough spot to be in.
>
> **You:** It's been really hard to deal with.
>
> **Friend:** I can hear how upset you are.

You: I wish I had more support.

Friend: Tell me more. I'm here to help.

What is your reaction to how this friend is responding? How did you feel reading these responses? How did these responses compare in terms of soothing or activating your nervous system?

Let's try a parent/child version of this:

Script A

Child: I wanted the blue one!

Parent: What's the big deal?

Child: It's my favorite!

Parent: You're being dramatic.

Child: (Cries)

Parent: You have to get over it.

Script B

Child: I wanted the blue one!

Parent: Aww man, that's so disappointing.

Child: It's my favorite!

Parent: I know how much you wanted it.

Child: (Cries)

Parent: Let me help you deal with this.

Although the child's response is the same in both scenarios, in script A, the child may learn that expressing their upset feelings is unwanted. In script B, the child may learn that talking to their parent about their feelings is helpful and supportive. With enough repetition and consistency, they may eventually learn to validate their own feelings for themselves!

What validation responses work for you and your child? Choose some to have in your back pocket:

→ Oh, how frustrating!

→ Yeah, I get how that would make you feel really upset.

→ It makes a lot of sense to me that you would be upset about that.

→ I can tell how hard this is for you.

→ What a tough feeling that must be.

→ Could you tell me more?

→ If that happened to me, I would be (mad, anxious, down, scared) too!

→ It's so disappointing to try so hard and not have it go your way.

→ I am so sorry!

→ Oh no!

→ No wonder you are upset.

→ It can feel hard when plans change.

→ What?!

→ Of course that's upsetting!

Tip: Sometimes just thinking a kind thought, like "Awww, she looks so miserable" or "My poor boy is falling apart" can make you look kind and caring. Our kids know us well and it helps them if our faces match our words!

HALT, CHILD VERSION

HALT stands for Hungry, Angry, Lonely, or Tired. If these states are active, it can be more difficult to handle stress or make good decisions. When adults feel this way, it's best to pause and regulate before making big decisions.

For children, these basics still apply; most of us know that if our child is especially hungry or tired, they have a harder time dealing with stress, are more fragile, and can tantrum. We suggest a slightly different version of HALT for children:

H: Hungry. Kids generally have low tolerance for being hungry and it makes them grumpy. For kids who aren't sensitive to their hunger cues, make sure your child pauses to have snacks. Plan ahead when you know your child needs to eat in order to feel regulated.

A: Angry or upset. Offer validation, co-regulation and/or physical soothing to help them talk about, process, or soothe their feelings.

L: Lacking connection or attention. Give them attention or connection.

T: Tired. Help them to soothe, relax, and get to sleep if needed.

REAL-LIFE EXAMPLE

"One time a very good friend was visiting for a week. During that week, on a morning when my five-year-old daughter and I would have normally been home together alone, she was really whiny and unpleasant. I was quite embarrassed. When my friend went out in the afternoon, my daughter instantly returned to her cheerful self and it was obvious that she had felt left out or lacking connection and attention. If I had just spent five minutes to focus on her and her needs, likely her mood would have been just fine. I could have said, 'I think you are feeling left out! I am sorry (with kisses!). Would you like to bring your puzzle over and I can help while I talk?'"

HELP CHILDREN TALK ABOUT THEIR FEELINGS

Helping children express themselves is an important coping skill for self-regulation. As Mr. Rogers says, "When we can talk about our feelings, they become less overwhelming, less upsetting, and less scary." The act of talking about feelings and being listened to by a supportive adult who expresses care and understanding can help kids feel better. Offering validating comments can often help kids keep talking and express more. This is a vital way people process emotions. Below are some gentle and direct ways to approach this topic with your kids.

Examples of probing/curious questions to use when child is upset*:

→ How did that make you feel?

→ Tell me more. What happened next?

→ What are you feeling?

→ Help me to understand your side of things.

→ What do you want me to know about this?

→ What was that like for you?

→ I might have a feeling of what you're going through.

→ Would you like my opinion or do you just want me to listen?

→ I am guessing you felt X... is that right?

→ I would feel X if that happened to me.

Choose two of the above to try out, and make a note of what feels like a good fit:

Choice 1: _____

Choice 2: _____

Talking about feelings can help a lot, but at first, it can feel daunting because it can hurt a little, and people worry about having to *feel* emotion. If adults avoid talking about feelings because it's hard, imagine how hard it can be for a child! It makes much more sense, in a child's mind, to pretend that certain feelings aren't there. It's awful to feel left out, different, jealous, or guilty, let alone to have to talk about these feelings. So, there are lots of good reasons children avoid this (Barish 2012). What you can share with your kids is that talking about feelings will never hurt a lot (no one has ever ended up in the hospital for talking about feelings!), and when you let your worries or sadness or anger off your chest with an adult that you trust, you can feel much better. BUT, for sure, it can hurt a little bit at first. The best way to combat this fear is to model emotional expression yourself.

---

* Exercise based on National Alliance on Mental Illness, "Validating & Invalidating Statements and Curious Questions." https://namibrevard.org/Information/Validating-and-Invalidating-Statements.pdf.

SHARING STORIES

Kids love hearing stories about their parents and the adults around them when they were kids themselves. When your child is going through something tough, it is especially helpful to know that someone they love and admire has been through the same thing, and how that person may have dealt with it and recovered from it.

Here are some pretty universal examples of hurt or upset feelings in children that can be soothed by adult stories with the same themes:

→ Having to practice a lot at something to get better at it

→ Being afraid of something before you've tried it

→ Losing a game/failing at something

Can you share a story with your child about a time in your own childhood when you felt big feelings? You can use this as a strategy for connection and co-regulation, as well as for helping your child talk about their feelings and learn ways to cope with them.

NAMING AND NOTICING FEELINGS

When adults model talking about feelings, it sets a good foundation for children being able to do so themselves.

Here are some examples adults can use:

→ I'm so frustrated that I burned the toast. I have to start again!

→ I'm feeling stressed that the bus is late.

→ I am so relieved that it didn't rain today!

Parents can then ask their child, "what was that like for you," or, "how did that make you feel?" See our section on modeling for more information (page 26).

USE OF ROUTINE, STRUCTURE, AND CONSISTENCY

Routines can help with regulation and internalizing rules and important life skills such as transitions and limits. This tool will set the foundation for healthy adult habits. This is true because all humans feel better when they know what to expect, and especially small ones, as they have very little control over their worlds. Additionally, whether we are monkeys or humans, we need to learn habits as youngsters that will help us survive in adulthood. By the age of five, your child's home life should be somewhat predictable to them (just like the school day is) and if there is something different going on, your child should be told in advance.

You are likely already using many routines in your day-to-day life. If you are not, the development of routines, structure, and consistency can be very supportive for both parent and child self-regulation.

Routines: Kids do much better with the same basic routines every day (wake-up, bedtime, meal times, after school routine). Aim to keep your routines as simple and consistent as possible.

Structure also may mean:

→ Insisting that kids ask for permission before taking a snack or engaging in an activity

→ Making important decisions at the parent level

→ Keeping language, music, and visual input (movies, the news, shows) age appropriate

Consistency may also mean:

→ Keeping routines in place and acknowledging when they are not and why

→ House rules (e.g., knocking on a door before opening it, use of manners, cleaning up after oneself)

→ Enforcing screen time allowance (when and for how long?)*

*For more support on structure and routine with screen time, see the resource Common Sense Media (www.commonsensemedia.org).

CAREGIVER EXERCISE

Reflect on a current aspect of your caregiver experiences and routines that may need some improvement (example: morning drop off routine, bedtime, making dinner, parent decompression time, parent-child connection time):

_____

_____

_____

_____

Imagine a better process and outcome of the scenario. How would you describe that?

_____

_____

_____

_____

Allow yourself to consider some practical ways to bridge the gap between your current routine and your wished for: what is within your control to change?

_____

_____

_____

_____

INTERVENTIONS FOR TRANSITIONS: USE ANTICIPATORY GUIDANCE

Five- through eight-year-old children still benefit from support with transitions. Many great plans fall apart because kids have not had enough information in advance. Planning ahead and offering what is called "anticipatory guidance" can be helpful for developing their tolerance for change.

A helpful approach is to use your words to prompt your children's thinking! For example:

→ We are going to grandma's house; what can you do if you get bored? Do you want to bring a few toys?

→ We are going to a restaurant for a special event; what can you do if you want to get out of your seat and look around like last time? Would it help if you sit near the other kids or near me?

Another option for supporting this skill is having a family calendar. You can take a moment to review it with your child and discuss what is happening for the day or the week. It should be on the wall where your children can look at it.

Parent exercise: Think of upcoming transitions or new experiences your child is facing. Write them here:

_____

_____

_____

Consider how you would talk about it with them using anticipatory guidance. When adults think ahead, kids can too!

CO-REGULATION WITH WORDS

Calming a child during a meltdown is very difficult, and you should not expect a child of this age to calm down right away. This is when you have to help them ride a wave of emotion as best you can. This is also when being patient, calm, and firm about physical boundaries is most important. These phrases support a child's regulation in the moment of an intense emotional upset because they allow a child to feel understood.

"You wish…"

→ you wish you could wear the shoes that you want instead of the shoes I am giving you to wear.

→ you wish we could stay up all night and never go to bed!

→ you wish X or Y were different.

"I hear you" or "I understand" or "I get it."

→ Child: I can't stand broccoli!
   Parent: I hear you.

→ Child: I am afraid to sleep without my missing stuffie!
   Parent: I understand.

→ Child: I really wanted to go to the park today!
   Parent: I get it.

Other helpful responses:

→ How can I help?

→ It's okay to feel sad.

→ We can handle this.

→ Let's slow down.

→ Let's get you a drink of ice water.

→ I know you are very upset. Let's sit on the couch together.

Add your own:

_____   _____

_____   _____

_____   _____

CO-REGULATION WITHOUT WORDS

As noted previously (see use of physical regulation strategies, page 84), sometimes it is best to use no words at all! Just your calm physical presence is enough to help your child calm themself. If your child is in a safe space, you can:

→ Sit nearby (many kids do not like to be cornered) and deep-breathe.

→ Focus on your own thoughts: _My child is just feeling upset. I can give them some space and some time._

→ Rub your child's back or feet (if welcome by the child).

→ Offer your eye contact and full presence.

→ Come down to your child's level and place a hand on their chest.

→ Listen without offering any advice.

→ Stay calm yourself (see Parent Self-Regulation Strategies in chapter 8).

→ Use mmmhhhs and nod your head.

It can also be helpful to just start walking, as children this age will usually follow you. If you have access to outside space, walking outdoors is wonderfully co-regulating. Eventually you might calmly take your child's hand.

CHAPTER 11

INTERVENTIONS FOR SPECIFIC SITUATIONS AND HIGH-EMOTION MOMENTS

HANDLING OUTBURSTS IN PUBLIC SPACES

Staying calm is always the goal. This way you show your child how to handle a challenging situation without losing your cool, as well as display your own steadiness in relation to their storms. When your child has an outburst, remember these tips:

→ Keep you and your child in a cocoon. Keep your focus on yourself and your child and imagine a glass dome around you both that makes you invisible and is also soundproof!

→ Keep in mind that adult passersby have either been there before and have empathy for you, feel supportive of you and your child, and/or hope that you can de-escalate the situation.

→ For those adults you feel judged by, know that you are the only one walking in your shoes. Stand firm in this perspective.

→ Internal script/How to talk self through it: "I am doing the best I can. Nothing terrible is happening to me or my child. I am just feeling self-conscious."

→ Try not to shame yourself or your child.

→ Come down to your child's level, use a soothing tone of voice, stay calm and firm about physical boundaries, and use your go-to strategies for co-regulation.

→ Use repair when some or all of the above has gone awry.

When you are with family or friends who are judgmental, try these tips:

→ Prepare ahead of time. Send a text to your family member: "Your grandson is really tired today. He might have a meltdown. It would be really helpful if you let me handle it."

→ Have a phrase that works: "I got this. We can talk more later!"

→ Move to a private place: "We will see you back here in 10 minutes."

Add your own:

_____

_____

_____

Circle the tips above that are helpful. Take a picture with your phone so you always have it handy.

WHAT TO SAY/THINK/DO AFTER LOSING YOUR COOL WITH YOUR CHILD

Please see our section on the importance of repair with your child (pages 18–22).

Here is some guidance:

1. First, provide repair for yourself. You can say, "Parenting is a difficult job that I do mostly well. Good parents can still make mistakes. All healthy relationships have moments of rupture and repair."

2. Then, repair with your child. Here are some simple steps to guide a repair:

   → Notice when you have calmed enough and have started to process your anger, shame, or guilt.

   → Consider what you would like to say to your child.

   → Say "I'm sorry" and link the apology to your behavior.

   → Offer a hug, high-five, or back rub if accepted.

   → Offer your child a chance to respond and share how they feel.

   → Be brief! Try not to talk too much or you may end up overexplaining, mistakenly blaming the child, making excuses, etc.

Notice if you are often having to make repairs. And if so, why?

DO'S	DON'TS
Engage in a repair as soon as possible.	Blame the child for your behavior (I got too angry because you made me upset).
Address the behavior or actions that you want to repair.	Expect your child to forgive/feel better.
Ask your child if they have questions or want to express their feelings about the rupture.	Force closeness or joke around.

PARENT SELF-REGULATION FOR INTENSIVE SITUATIONS

Here we pull together all of the de-escalation and parent self-regulation strategies we have already discussed for an easy reference:

→ When you feel that you're escalating, one of the best strategies in these moments is to do *nothing* (when you are surrounded by bricks, stand still!).

→ Take some time to regroup. If you can, let your child know you need a moment to calm yourself and that you will be back.

→ Pass the Baton: If another calm adult is present, see if you can trade places for a moment, letting that adult know you need some time to regulate.

→ Coach yourself with self-talk:

- My child is having a hard time; it's temporary.

- My only goal is to remain calm.

- I can get through this.

- My child's tantrum will pass as I remain calm.

- My child and I will ride out this tough moment.

- Doing nothing right now is my best option.

- I am doing the best I can.

- Nothing terrible is happening to me or my child. I am just feeling self-conscious.

- Say to yourself, "My anger in this moment is not worth harming the relationship with my child."

Add your own to this list:

_____

_____

_____

_____

_____

PART 3
ACTIVITIES FOR PARENTS AND KIDS

CHAPTER 12

KIDS ARE AMAZING

This section is for parents and kids! Parents, lead your child through these activities that introduce concepts and engage kids in self-regulation practice.

AMAZING KIDS

Kids are capable of amazing things. They can even change the world! One of the amazing things about you is that at your age, your brain is what's called "plastic;" it can change and grow and stretch. This means your brain is at one of the most creative times in your entire life! At this age, you are much better than adults at using your imagination, exploring, and inventing.

Here are descriptions of some amazing five- to eight-year-old children throughout time. Read below to learn more:

Wolfgang Amadeus Mozart: Eight Years Old

Did you know that one of the most well-known composers of all time was just five years old when he composed his first song on the piano? As a child from a very musical family, Wolfgang learned to master 10 musical instruments, including the harpsichord and the violin. At six years old, he went on a tour across Europe. Just as impressive, at the age of eight, he composed his first symphony! The rest is musical history. Wolfgang shows us that eight-year-olds can be full of talent and determination!

Ruby Bridges: Six Years Old

Six-year-old Ruby was the first Black child to integrate the formerly all-White William Franz School in Louisiana in 1960. The taunts and threats against her were so bad, she had to be escorted to her class by federal marshals. Ruby completed her education and became an icon of the American Civil Rights Movement. Ruby shows us that at even six years old, you can be incredibly brave and inspiring.

Shirley Temple: Six Years Old

After entering show business at the tender age of three, Shirley Temple worked as a film actress, making eight movies by age six! Her naturally cheery demeanor and amazing talent made her a superstar and showed the world that, no matter what your age, you can be incredibly successful. Shirley shows us that six-year-olds can be powerful and uplift others.

What are some amazing things about you? Can you think of a time you were brave, showed talent, or inspired someone?

_____

_____

_____

_____

_____

_____

_____

AMAZING KIDS TALKING ABOUT HOW THEY CALM DOWN

Here are some other amazing kids talking about how they calm down:

Greta (age eight)

Can you think of a time when you were really upset?

Yes, today, when I had an argument with my friends.

How old were you?

Eight, today.

What happened?

They gave each other signs and wanted to go into a certain room.

What were you feeling (it could be more than one feeling)?

I felt excluded.

How big was that feeling(s) (1 is the smallest, 5 is the biggest)?

3.

How did you calm yourself down?

I didn't calm myself down, I went to them and said: "Let's be friends again."

Do you have any ideas to help other kids when they are very sad or angry or hurt?

You could ask: Can I help you, or are you alright?

Yoli (age five)

Can you think of a time when you were really upset?

When I couldn't find my scissors.

How old were you?

Five.

What happened?

I was making a card for mommy and I couldn't find my scissors. I looked for them and couldn't find them.

What were you feeling? (It could be more than one feeling.)

Mad.

How big was that feeling(s) (1 is the smallest, 5 is the biggest)?

3/in the middle

How did you calm yourself down?

I looked for my scissors and found them.

Do you have any ideas to help other kids when they are very sad or angry or hurt?

Give them a hug.

Cy (age seven)

Can you think of a time when you were really upset?

Thinking we were leaving Brooklyn and all our stuff would stay there.

How old were you?

Seven and 3/4 years old.

What happened?

I started to cry.

What were you feeling? (It could be more than one feeling.)

Sad and scared and angry.

How big was that feeling(s) (1 is the smallest, 5 is the biggest)?

5.

How did you calm yourself down?

Talking about it calmed me down.

Do you have any ideas to help other kids when they are very sad or angry or hurt?

Breathing and talking about your feelings can help other kids.

Alice (age six)

Can you think of a time when you were really upset?

When my sister and I were playing and then she knocked something down really special that took me 10 minutes to do, and then she just knocked it over!

How old were you?

Six.

What happened?

We were playing dolls, there were babies and then—it wasn't on purpose, she turned around and everything fell!

What were you feeling? (It could be more than one feeling.)

So sad and mad and angry and frustrated!

How big was that feeling(s) (1 is the smallest, 5 is the biggest)?

3 and 4.

How did you calm yourself down?

Well, I didn't really calm myself down cause I was so frustrated, so I ran to my mom. And then she told me, "Take a deep breath," and I had already walked away from the problem.

Do you have any ideas to help other kids when they are very sad or angry or hurt?

Take a deep breath. A deeeeeep breath. And the second idea: walk away from the problem.

Alexis (age eight)

Can you think of a time when you were really upset?

I was really upset when... that's a tough one, I've gotten upset a lot of times. But it's hard to remember the times I got upset. Oh wait, probably the time when my sister was on the monkey bars and she fell down and her nose got bloody.

How old were you?

Seven.

What happened?

I was playing a game with my friends and we had to leave the park early because my sister's nose was bleeding.

What were you feeling? (It could be more than one feeling).

I was feeling a little bit upset and sorry for my sister that her nose was bleeding.

How big was that feeling(s) (1 is the smallest, 5 is the biggest)?

3 or 2.

How did you calm yourself down?

Well, first, I asked my sister if is she was okay 'cause if she was actually really hurt then I wouldn't even have been mad that I had to leave. But she was fine except her nose was bleeding. I just took breaths and we went home and then my sister blowed her nose. Then we watched some TV and had a snack and then did some homework I think.

Do you have any ideas to help other kids when they are very sad or angry or hurt?

First you can ask them if they are okay or maybe if you have an idea to help them you can tell them some recommendations or tell them a story of when you were scared and how you calmed down.

Taha (age five)

Can you think of a time when you were really upset?

Every time I'm in the dark.

How old were you?

Five.

What happened?

I think there's a monster. In my head I see a monster.

What were you feeling? (It could be more than one feeling.)

It makes me want to run away.

How big was that feeling(s) (1 is the smallest, 5 is the biggest)?

2.

How did you calm yourself down?

When I'm scared I fight the monsters in my head and I turn on the light. Do you know how I fight the monsters in my head? I turn on the light and then they suffer. If I can't turn on the light I fight them in my head.

Do you have any ideas to help other kids when they are very sad or angry or hurt?

They can ask: Can I have some cold water please?

Alioune (age eight)

Can you think of a time when you were really upset?

Yes, when my friends were beating me up with their jackets.

How old were you?

I was eight.

What happened?

They took off their jackets and they started whipping me with the zipper, then I punched one of them in the eye.

What were you feeling? (It could be more than one feeling.)

I was sad and I was angry.

How big was that feeling(s) (1 is the smallest, 5 is the biggest)?

The frustration was the biggest, a 5.

How did you calm yourself down?

I didn't. Well, I was just breathing. I thought of my favorite animals. Pitbulls and other dogs.

Do you have any ideas to help other kids when they are very sad or angry or hurt?

Think of a fluffy dog.

Lena (age five)

Can you think of a time when you were really upset?

Well when my little sister bites me I freak out!

How old were you?

Four I guess?

What happened?

We were playing and fighting over Barbie Dolls in the tub and she bit me.

What were you feeling? (It could be more than one feeling.)

I was feeling like ugh! Why did you bite me! I'm so terrified right now! Like why did you do this? I am angry, aargh! Like when those blue people came in *Inside Out* and Joy was dragging anger.

How big was that feeling(s) (1 is the smallest, 5 is the biggest)?

Can I say 8?

How did you calm yourself down?

It was like when you [mom] came in the bathroom and I felt oh, it's so relaxing, oh, I am grateful now that mom's here right now.

Do you have any ideas to help other kids when they are very sad or angry or hurt?

Yeah. Hugging. I can ask them; if they just ignore me then I'm not gonna hug them. If a kid is angry I don't know what I could do. Maybe I would just not do anything. I would just let them relax 'til they're alright.

Now it is your turn!

Can you think of a time when you were really upset?

_____
_____
_____
_____
_____
_____
_____

How old were you?

_____
_____

What happened?

_____
_____
_____
_____
_____
_____
_____

What were you feeling? (It could be more than one feeling.)

_____

_____

_____

_____

How big was that feeling(s) (1 is the smallest, 5 is the biggest)?

_____

_____

_____

_____

How did you calm yourself down?

_____

_____

_____

_____

Do you have any ideas to help other kids when they are very sad or angry or hurt?

_____

_____

_____

_____

_____

_____

_____

DOES BREATHING HELP YOU CALM DOWN?

Cy and Alice say breathing helps them calm down when they are upset. Does it help you? See page 129 for more on breathing and calming down your body.

Yoli said a hug helps kids calm down. Do hugs help you when you have a big feeling?

_____

_____

_____

Lena said hugs would NOT help with angry feelings. Do you agree or disagree?

_____

_____

_____

Why?

_____

_____

_____

_____

_____

_____

_____

_____

_____

_____

_____

_____

CHAPTER 13

ALL ABOUT THINKING, TALKING ABOUT, AND FEELING FEELINGS

A Letter from Your Feelings

Dear kid:

Have you ever laughed so hard you fell down and started rolling on the ground? Cried when you lost a game? Got embarrassed when you made a mistake or tripped in front of someone? Gotten so mad you threw something? Became so frustrated that you couldn't calm down, no matter how hard a grown-up tried to help you? Well then, guess what? You are a kid with normal, healthy feelings.

The book you are reading right now is called The Self-Regulation Workbook for Children Ages 5 to 8. What is self-regulation? Self-regulation is understanding your feelings. It also means learning all the ways you react to us so that you can make choices about how you behave. You have help inside of you (your own body and mind) and outside of you (your grown-up) to help with big feelings. What is a big feeling? When you feel really, really mad, sad, happy, scared, or frustrated, just to name a few. When you feel these feelings, sometimes you can have a BIG reaction, like a tantrum or throwing or hitting something. Another word for feelings is emotions.

Emotions are different from feelings in your body like hunger, pain, sleepiness, or having to go to the bathroom. Most kids have had a lot of experiences with these (hopefully not too many of the pain kind, though). But as you probably already know, emotions also make you feel something in your body and your mind. You can actually feel feelings!

Feelings: you are supposed to FEEL us! But do feelings ever feel TOO big or take too long to go away, or make you feel like you will never feel happy again? When feelings feel too big, grown-ups can help, and you can even learn how to help yourself. If you want to learn more about how to help yourself with big feelings, this section of the book is perfect for you.

Even though feelings can feel BIG in your body and your mind, we can never hurt you, like a bee sting or scraping your knee. But we can make you feel a bit heartbroken (when you are disappointed about something), or full of butterflies (when you are nervous), or like you are about to explode (when you are so excited!). This is all normal too.

You have feelings because you are a real person, not a robot! You are a mammal, and all mammals have feelings! Your feelings make sure you know all the parts of who you are—the parts of you that get mad and sad and happy. All of these different parts of you are so important. Remember, feelings will always pass and feelings will never make you sick. *All* people have feelings, big and small. Feel free to write us back!

Love,

Your feelings

Now that you know more about feelings, let's try some activities.

HOW DOES IT FEEL?

Imagine you just broke your favorite toy or lost your favorite thing (oh no!). What does that feel like? Share it with your grown-up using your words or a picture.

Now read the responses below and see how you would feel if your parent responded this way:

Parent A: I told you not to leave it on the floor! You should have listened to me!

Parent B: Oh no! You can just get another one.

Parent C: Oh sweetie, your favorite. I am so sorry that happened! Let me give you a big hug.

How do you feel about how each parent responded?

_____

_____

_____

_____

_____

_____

_____

_____

_____

Which response would have helped you the most?

_____

_____

_____

_____

_____

_____

_____

_____

_____

What would you like your parent to say if you were in this situation?

_____

_____

_____

_____

_____

_____

_____

_____

_____

Now imagine your parent is really late to pick you up after school and you are feeling nervous and upset. What does that feel like? Share it with your grown-up.

Here's how three different responses might sound like when a parent arrives for pick-up.

Parent A: There was so much traffic! C'mon, let's go.

Parent B: Sorry I'm late!

Parent C: Are you okay dear (gives a big hug)? You look upset.

How do you feel about how each parent responded?

_____

_____

_____

_____

_____

_____

_____

_____

_____

_____

_____

Which response would have helped you the most?

_____

_____

_____

_____

_____

_____

_____

_____

What would you like your parent to say if you were in this situation?

_____

_____

_____

_____

_____

_____

_____

_____

_____

CAN YOU IMAGINE?

Now let's see if you can imagine what someone else would be thinking or feeling. When we do this, we can practice knowing our own emotions better. Special note: there are no right or wrong answers, you can just make your best guess.

A child is expecting to go to a special event with their parent. Their parent says they have to cancel because of a work meeting. What is this child thinking and feeling?

_____

_____

_____

_____

_____

_____

_____

A child's favorite teacher announces that she is pregnant and that the class will have a substitute teacher for the rest of the school year. What is this child thinking and how does this child feel?

_____

_____

_____

_____

_____

_____

_____

GUESS THE FEELING

Have your parent write down different feeling words on slips of paper or note cards and put them into a hat or shoebox. Now pick out the feeling and act it out only with your body language and facial expressions. See if the other person can guess the feeling!

You can pick any feelings you like, but here are a few to ideas to choose from:

→ Surprise

→ Disappointment

→ Scared

→ Mad

→ Frustrated

→ Happy

→ Sad

→ Bored

GUESS WHO?

Pretend to be a member of your family or extended family. Act out this person using facial expressions and body language. You can pretend to be this person while they are going about their normal day. See if your family member can guess who you are acting as.

Animals Have Feelings Too

Did you know that animals have feelings too? Do you have a pet at home? What helps them to calm down? How can you tell if your pet is happy or sad? If they could talk, what would they say? How does your pet tend to calm you down or make you upset?

FEELINGS ARE SUPERPOWERS

Did you know that feelings are meant to help us? If you think about it, all feelings can help us in some way. Here are some examples:

→ **Anger:** Helps us notice something that really bothers us: "I don't like it when you take my toy." Anger also helps us to stand up for ourselves, or for someone else: "Hey! That's not fair!"

→ **Sadness:** When we show that we are sad or upset, adults can tell that we need help and will try to support us. It shows our grown-ups that we need a hug.

→ **Disappointment:** When we are disappointed, first we feel sad and down for a bit. Then we have the power to think really hard and imagine a solution or alternative to the thing we are disappointed about.

So, feelings are sort of like superpowers. They help us figure things out, get help, and stand up for ourselves! Here are more ways to use your powers:

→ **Patience power:** When you are waiting calmly for something you really want

→ **Frustration power:** When you are really frustrated about something and you can use your words, not your body to express it

→ **Pausing power:** When you can catch yourself before you do or say something you may regret later

Challenge: teach your grown-up about one of these powers and see if they can use it!

FEELINGS ARE LIKE CRAYONS... THEY COME IN MANY DIFFERENT COLORS!

Have you ever heard someone say they feel "blue"? This means they are feeling sad or down. There! We just used three words to express the same feeling. Can you find the three words? What feeling is it?

Just as we showed, there can be many words to express just *one* type of feeling. For example, when someone feels happy, they can also say they feel cheerful, delighted, or carefree! These words are like using all the different colors in a crayon box. Just like drawing, when you need just the right color, sometimes it helps to use just the right word to express your feelings.

Use this list to help you figure out the name of your feeling:

MAD	SAD	EXCITED	HAPPY
Angry	Gloomy	Thrilled	Peaceful
Furious	Glum	Pumped Up	Hunky-Dory
Enraged	Blue	Eager	Chill
Fuming	Down	Electric	A-Okay
Seeing Red	Low	Buzzing	Awesome
Berserk	Unhappy	Over the Moon	Terrific
	Awful		Pleased
	Miserable		

> In the United Kingdom, people say they feel "cross" when they are mad about something.

Does your family have special words to express certain feelings? See what it's like for you and your family to try out some new words to express your feelings!

MAKE UP YOUR OWN WORD FOR HOW YOU FEEL

What's a made-up word you can make for when:

You are nervous about something?

_____

_____

_____

You are excited about something?

_____

_____

_____

What about when you are nervous AND excited about something?

_____

_____

_____

The **SELF-REGULATION** Workbook for Children Ages 5 to 8

What's a made-up word you can make for when:

You are sad about something?

_____

- -

_____

You are mad about something?

_____

- -

_____

You are sad AND mad about something?

_____

- -

_____

As you can see, it's also true that you can have two feelings at once! This happens all the time. For example, we use the term "bittersweet" when we feel a mix of happy and sad at the same time, like you are really happy when you finish first grade, but you may also be a little sad, because you have to say good-bye to your teacher!

Let's use the words we listed before and see what happens when we put them together. Draw a line between two words and see what you come up with!

Peaceful	Glum	A-Okay	Awful
Angry	Pumped Up	Fuming	Buzzing
Gloomy	Chill	Down	Terrific
Thrilled	Enraged	Electric	Berserk!
Hunky-Dory	Blue	Awesome	Miserable
Furious	Eager	Seeing Red	Over the Moon

Write down your favorite match here:

_____

- -

_____

Can you imagine a time you would ever feel this way?

_____

- -

_____

- -

_____

THIS SELF-TALK VS. THAT SELF-TALK

We all have thoughts in our minds. These thoughts can be helpful or they can make us feel worse! Sometimes you just have to be sad or mad for a little while in order to feel better. Other times, we can feel a little sad or mad at first, and then, if we can figure out how to "self-talk," it can help us feel much better.

When hard things happen, circle the self-talk that would make you feel better:

→ You swing and miss the ball:
   "I am terrible at this!" *or* "I can try again!"

→ You get the answer wrong in class:
   "I don't know anything!" *or* "It's okay that I am still learning this!"

→ You rip your new favorite shirt:
   "I can ask my dad to fix it." *or* "It is ruined."

→ Your friend invites someone else over for a playdate:
   "I guess he wants to have more than one friend. I have other friends too. My other friends are..." *or* "He doesn't like me anymore."

Ask your grown-up about something wrong or upsetting that happened in their day. What self-talk did they use?

You can also use "self-talk" when you want to be your own cheerleader or helper. You can say things like "I am frustrated, but I know I can wait my turn" (Novick and Novick 2010).

CHAPTER 14

HOW TO HANDLE IT: SELF-CONTROL AND FRUSTRATION

What is self-control?

Self-control is a really good and powerful feeling. It helps you *not* do the thing you really might feel like doing (throwing, yelling, hitting), because you know it could make things worse. It also helps you to *do* the thing that may be hard to do but will be the better choice. It's when you tell your body and mind: you can handle this or stop! The thing that your body wants to do is so powerful, it even has its own word: "impulse." Self-control is how your mind controls impulses (what your body or feelings want to do). Self-control is one of our emotional superpowers.

Did you know that you have already used self-control, maybe even today? Check this list to see when you have used self-control:

- ❏ Waiting your turn when you are really excited to participate
- ❏ Thanking someone for a present you don't like
- ❏ Losing a game, then playing again
- ❏ Trying again after making a mistake
- ❏ Keeping a promise, even if you don't want to
- ❏ Passing by a delicious-looking big piece of cake and not eating it
- ❏ Accepting "no" for an answer
- ❏ Waiting for something that you really want
- ❏ Asking before you do something
- ❏ Practicing something like sports, music, or dance
- ❏ Waiting quietly for a long time at the doctor's office
- ❏ Saying "no thank you!" instead of *yuck!* when someone offers you a food you don't like
- ❏ Swallowing a medicine you need when you are sick, even if it tastes awful

- ❏ Waiting for someone to pass you a toy instead of grabbing it from their hands
- ❏ Trying something new that you are a bit nervous about
- ❏ Playing fairly during a card game, even if you really want to cheat
- ❏ Doing homework before playing games
- ❏ Not eating a second dessert when you are already full
- ❏ Choosing the second-best flavor of ice cream if there is none of your favorite
- ❏ Telling the truth, even if you think you may get in trouble
- ❏ Eating just a little of your dinner, even when you don't like it

There are times when it may be easier or harder to use self-control. The good news is, the more you use self-control (at home, at school, with your friends and your family), the better you can become at it.

THE STANFORD MARSHMALLOW EXPERIMENT

What would you do if someone gave you a cookie and said that you could either eat it right away, or if you waited 15 minutes to eat it, you could have two cookies? Would you eat the cookie right away, or would you wait, knowing you could get two?

This experiment was done at Stanford University in California. It studies something called "delayed gratification." This means the ability to wait for something you really want.

In this experiment, kids aged three to five years old were offered a special treat like a marshmallow that they could have right away *or* more of that same treat if they waited for a little while. The kids were left alone in the room with the treat while the researcher watched to see what would happen. Would the child eat the treat in front of them right away? Would they be able to sit 15 minutes, knowing that if they waited, they could get more? What do you think happened?

One of the interesting things that the researchers observed was all of the different ways the kids in the experiment tried to deal with the feeling of waiting for a treat, one that was sitting right before their very eyes:

> "They made up quiet songs... hid their head in their arms, pounded the floor with their feet... a little girl rested her head, sat limply, relaxed herself, and proceeded to fall sound asleep" (Mischel et al. 1972).

So, these kids did all types of things (these are called strategies): covered their eyes, talked to themselves, made up games with their hands and feet, and sang, to name a few.

What were the results?

Surprisingly, the results showed that thinking about (and even seeing) a reward you are waiting for makes it *harder* to wait for it! *Not* thinking about a reward helps you with the feeling of waiting for it. To make it easier for you to deal with waiting for something you really want, it is best to try to distract yourself or find a way not to think about it. So, the key to dealing with this kind of situation is to figure out ways to make it less frustrating. Using a distraction such as creating a game, moving your body, or even talking to yourself may help with dealing with the frustration of waiting for something you may want.

Now, your turn. Try your own experiment!

Ask your parent to put a treat you really like on a plate in front of you. Know that you can get another one if you wait a bit. Use a timer to keep track. As you are waiting to eat your treat, what helps?

Write down all of the things you tried and circle whether or not they helped:

_____ Yes/No

_____ Yes/No

_____ Yes/No

_____ Yes/No

What strategies worked? Which didn't? Did you wait out the time?!

FRUSTRATION CAN BE... FUN?

Frustration is a really tough feeling to deal with, and we can get frustrated for many reasons. The feeling of not getting something right is tough! When you try and try and it still doesn't work, it hurts! Our brains can get a bit tired and want to give up!

We can even get mad at ourselves, other people, or the thing we are doing because it is not going well. It's normal to feel this way at times; everyone has.

What's on the other side of frustration? Well, when you've been frustrated, then you keep trying, have you ever learned something new? Figured something out? Felt proud or relieved? Sometimes we need to be frustrated in order to grow.

REAL-LIFE EXAMPLE

When my son was seven, he learned to ride a bike in *one* day. Great, right? Well this day was *full* of tough moments and frustration, even a little bit of blood, sweat, and tears (it was a really hot day). Even though he was really frustrated (and truthfully, so was I), he kept trying, and eventually, he got it! He was so incredibly proud, relieved and happy. I was too!

A good way to practice dealing with frustration is to try to do something a little challenging that can also be fun. Do your best to read these tongue twisters without making any mistakes. If you keep making a mistake, notice how you feel. Do you want to quit, or try again? How does it feel when you get the whole thing right? With this exercise, your body can get a mini practice in feeling and dealing with frustration!

Directions: Repeat these tongue twisters without making a mistake. If you make a mistake, start from the beginning.

Woodchuck

How much wood would a woodchuck chuck if a woodchuck could chuck wood?

Sally Sells Seashells

Sally sells seashells by the seashore.

She sells seashells on the seashell shore.

The seashells she sells are seashore shells,

Of that I'm sure.

Peter Piper

Peter Piper picked a peck of pickled peppers,

A peck of pickled peppers Peter Piper picked;

If Peter Piper picked a peck of pickled peppers,

Where's the peck of pickled peppers Peter Piper picked?

BRAIN EXERCISES TO DEAL WITH FRUSTRATION?[2]

Here's an experiment to try out. Try each of the actions below, one at a time:

→ Rub your belly in circular motion and pat your head.

→ Draw the number eight with your finger in the air but use your left finger if you are right-handed and right finger if you are left-handed.

→ Draw a triangle with your right hand, whether in the air or on a piece of paper. At the same time, draw a circle with your left hand.

→ Make your left hand do a sawing motion and your right a hammering motion.

Having done these brain exercises, try the tongue twisters again! Are they harder to do? Easier?

Now try one of these breathing tools:

→ **Pizza Breath:** Imagine your hand is a slice of delicious-looking pizza. First, take a moment to smell the delicious slice. Imagine toppings if you like them. Take a nice, long, deep breath, breathing in the smell of the imaginary pizza. Then, take a moment to gently blow on the hot slice. Exhale through your mouth. Take a nice, long, slow, gentle breath to cool it off. Make sure the exhale is longer than the inhale you took to smell the toppings. Repeat this a few times to allow your body to calm down.

→ **Flower Breath:** Pretend your fist is a beautiful, wonderful-smelling flower. First, take a moment to smell the amazing scent. Does it smell like a rose? Like vanilla? Like coconut? Take a nice, long, deep breath in through your nose, breathing in the smell of the imaginary flower. Then, take a moment to gently blow the petals of the flower. Exhale through your mouth. Take a nice, long, slow, gentle breath to blow off the petals of the flower. Make sure the exhale is longer than the inhale you took to smell the flower. Repeat!

→ **Bunny Rabbit Breaths:** Try breathing like a little bunny. Take three quick sniffs through your nose and then one looooong exhale. You can pretend you are sniffing for carrots! Repeat at least three times.

For all of these breathing strategies, remember to practice them at times you are already feeling calm so that you know how to use them well when you have a big feeling. Try one of these breathing tricks to help you the next time you are trying to calm down.

Caregivers, see other breathing strategies to teach your child from Martha Straus' wonderful book, *Cool, Calm, and Collected.*

---

2   Paul Dennison and Gail Dennison, *Brain Gym, Teachers Edition* (Edu-Kinesthetics, 1994).

Having tried these breathing exercises, try the tongue twisters again. Is it the same? Different? How?

Sometimes when we are frustrated, the best thing we can do is take a break. When we try the thing again, it may feel less frustrating.

So when you are dealing with something that is frustrating you can:

→ Keep trying and see if you learn or grow.

→ Take a break and try it again.

→ Try a brain or breathing exercise.

Go ahead and see which of these helps you the most when you are frustrated.

CHAPTER 15

HOW TO HELP YOUR BODY DEAL WITH BIG EMOTIONS

Our bodies give us signals. When we are hungry, our stomachs growl. When we are tired, our eyes may feel heavy.

The same goes for emotions! When we are sad, our bodies can feel heavy, and we may start to cry. When we are worried or nervous, it may feel like a million butterflies in our stomach. When we are mad, our faces may get hot, and we may want to hit or throw. When we are excited, we may want to jump up and down!

These signals are called "sensations," and they are clues as to what emotions we are feeling. When you recognize these sensations in your body, it can help you understand what you are feeling.

A lot of scientists have studied the connection between the mind, the body, and our feelings. We now know that when we have big emotions, not only can we help ourselves by using our minds, but we can also learn how to feel calmer by breathing and using our five senses.

There is nothing wrong with having big emotions. We all have them from time to time. Here are some ways to use your body to help you when you have very big emotions (see page 127):

→ Pizza Breath

→ Flower Breath

→ Bunny Rabbit Breaths

> **Hey kids!** One of the best ways to learn calming breaths is for YOU to teach your grown-up how to do it. Choose your favorite to teach to your grown-up.

Anger and frustration are similar, they both make you want to push, throw, and pound! One good way to deal with these feelings is to try something with your hands, feet, or voice:

1. Use both hands and push as hard as you can into a wall.

2. Stomp three times.

3. Do one big growl.

If you sometimes hit when you get mad, you can try practicing this skill:

1. Take three steps back from the thing that is making you mad.

2. Cross your arms and clench your fists.

3. Shout "I'm mad!"

4. Only put your hands down when you don't feel like hitting anymore.

You can also try putting the hitting feeling in your mouth, and saying it out loud:

→ I really want to kick right now but I won't!

→ I really want to hit right now but I'm going to get the teacher.

→ I really want to hit! Mom, can you help me?

Note: you have to practice this *a lot* of times until your body and mind knows just what to do, but you can do it!

Another option is to smell something so good, it helps your mind and body relax! Ask your parent to find you something you love to smell, like peppermint, or lavender, or cinnamon in a dried or essential oil form. Use a cloth, some cotton balls, and some string to create a good-smelling little pouch for you to breathe in for relaxation. Put a few drops of the scent on the cotton balls and then tie them up in the cloth to make a pouch.

What Is a Strategy?

Big feelings do not stay forever and ever. Feelings are like waves. They get smaller, all on their own, without you having to do anything about them. But did you know that there are many, many things you can do to help a big feeling get a bit smaller and feel better? These are called strategies. Sometimes just knowing that you have a strategy can help you with big feelings and problems.

Adults use strategies all the time. Here are some examples:

Kahlila: "If I am running late for an appointment, I get very stressed. One strategy that works for me is to call the place I am going or the person I am meeting and letting them know I am running late. Another strategy is to say to myself, 'Well, it's not the end of the world if I am a few minutes late.' Both of these strategies help me a lot."

Sarah: "When I am worried about something at night that may or may not happen the next day, I think to myself, 'The other people involved are sleeping now so there is no use in thinking about my worry now. I will think about it tomorrow when we are all awake!'"

Not only do we use strategies as adults, we also used strategies when we were kids like you!

REAL-LIFE EXAMPLES FROM THE AUTHORS

Kahlila: When I was eight, my older cousin told me about a movie she saw with a very scary monster. Even though I had not seen the movie myself and I knew monsters were not real, her description scared me so much. I had trouble going to sleep at night, and I would replay the scary scenes in my mind! Using my imagination, I decided that I would show this monster kindness and be his best and only friend. That way, he would never hurt me. This worked perfectly! Once I figured this out in my mind, I was never afraid of this monster again, and could go to sleep without worrying.

Sarah: When I was five, I had a lot of nightmares. It really helped me sleep to touch a very soft blanket in my bed that I loved and to say the name of something or someone I really loved, such as, "candy, candy, candy" or "mom, mom, mom."

As you may have noticed from the examples above, all people worry more at night. That is because we are tired and not as distracted as we are in the daytime. If you have worries at night, it might help to say to yourself, "I am just tired!"

The amazing kids we heard from earlier also used strategies to help with their feelings:

→ Greta spoke to the people who hurt her feelings...

→ Yoli kept looking for the thing she lost until she found it...

→ Cy talked about his upset feelings...

→ Alexis asked her sister if she was okay, then took some deep breaths...

→ Alice walked away from the problem and went to her mom...

→ Taha used his imagination to deal with the monsters in his head and turned on the light...

→ Alioune thought about his favorite animals to help him with his frustration...

→ Lena let herself feel relaxed and grateful when her mom came to help her...

→ Young Kahlila used her imagination and made the monster her friend...

→ Young Sarah thought about something she loved and held something comfy...

Strategies are ideas and actions that help. You probably already know a lot of them. What are some strategies you can use when:

You lose or break something you love:

_____

_____

_____

_____

_____

You are afraid to try a new food:

_____

_____

_____

_____

_____

You are so mad that your sibling took one of your toys to play with:

_____

_____

_____

_____

_____

_____

_____

_____

Repairing

This strategy is great to use AFTER you've had a big feeling and you may have done or said something you wish you had not (like throwing, hitting, or saying or doing something that hurt someone's feelings). Instead of just feeling upset about what happened, you can repair.

How to Repair

When you get mad at your parent, sibling, or friend and you do something you wish you could take back, do you know that there is something to help that person feel better? It's called a repair. Just like when we break something and fix it, a repair is when we may have hurt someone's feelings and then do or say something that lets them know we care about them.

Examples of how a kid can repair:

→ If you get very angry and hit or kick your sibling, you could repair it by saying that you are sorry and getting them an ice pack. Then you can say that next time, you will use your words to express your feelings.

→ If you leave out a friend at school, you can tell them you are sorry. Then you can explain why you did it. For example, you might say that you were feeling nervous when you were playing a game that you aren't good at and you got distracted.

To sum it up, here are all the things you can do when you are having a big feeling:

→ Remember: there is help from inside and outside of you.

→ You can use a strategy.

→ You can find the just-right words.

→ You can use your feelings as a superpower.

→ You can use self-control.

→ You can self-talk.

→ You can move your body.

→ You can take some deep breaths.

→ You can talk about the thing that is bothering you.

→ You can feel your feeling and ride it like a wave, knowing it will get smaller.

→ You can ask for help.

→ You can use your imagination to feel better about something.

→ You can repair.

Also remember, as you get bigger, your body and mind will continue to help you with big feelings. The more you practice as a kid, the better you can be at dealing with big feelings as an adult!

DRAWING FEELINGS AND PLAYING TOGETHER WITH ART

1. Try the Squiggle Game

The game is played as follows: the parent draws a squiggle and the child is asked to make a picture using the parent's squiggle. Next, the child begins the game and the parent makes a picture from the child's squiggle, trading back and forth. You can ask your child what they drew or what they think you drew.

2. Exquisite Corpse Drawing Activity

This is a fun collaborative drawing activity that can be done with two or three people. At the end, you reveal a new creation!

Take a piece of paper and divide it into three equal parts horizontally (fold one side one third of the way in the middle then fold the remaining third into the middle). Unfold your paper to reveal the three equal parts.

Now, it's time to draw. The first person draws the head. Once the head is done, fold it back so that it is hidden from the second person drawing. The second person draws the torso. Do not worry about matching up exactly to the head! You can connect each part to each other at the end. Make sure to fold over the torso so that the next person cannot see it. The third person (or, with two people, back to the first person) draws the legs and feet. Feel free to use different colors and designs to make each section unique!

When each section is done, unfold your paper to reveal the entire drawing. What does your creature look like?!

3. My Life Timeline

This activity helps children put things into perspective and gives you more information about how previous events have impacted them emotionally.

Take a stack of large index cards and have your child draw out life events such as the first day of school, a move, the birth of a sibling, a broken arm, or anything else that seems significant. Over time, you will have a stack of cards that can be laid out on the ground in a timeline. For example, "This is me when I was four years old visiting our new house before we moved in."

(Optional: For each drawing, on the bottom or back, have the child write: This is _____. I felt ___. And then have them rank the feeling from 1 to 5.)

WEATHER REPORT[3]

Have your child sit up with their back facing you or lying down on their stomach. Now begin talking about the weather that day and gently re-create the climate on their back, using your hands. For example, for a sunny day, you may make a fist and gently press it on their upper back or shoulder, mimicking the bright sun. For a windy day, you can move your hands and fingers playfully across their back. For a rainy day, you can move your fingers in a pitter patter motion from the top of their back to the bottom. You can combine any and all of these patterns to create a relaxing back rub and connect with your child at the end of the day.

EMOTIONS ARE LIKE WAVES

Here's a short story you can use at bedtime to teach kids about the nature of emotions. Bonus: use ocean sounds from your cell phone to enhance storytelling!

Imagine a beautiful day at the beach. The sky is clear and the air is light and breezy. You see the perfect-sized waves for surfing. You think of taking a nice ride on a wave. You head out to the water and jump on your surfboard. At first, you notice the gentle up and down motion of the waves. They have a steady rhythm that allows you to jump on top of your board. You hop on your surfboard and steady yourself. A big wave starts to approach. You feel your heart beating a bit faster and your body getting a little tense. As the wave gets closer, your whole body and mind is focused on it. You make it to the wave and are able to hop on! This wave is so big and so powerful! It's hard to keep yourself balanced on the surfboard, and you worry that you will fall off. For a long while it feels like the wave is going on and on, with its powerful force. A little nervous, you find yourself at the very top of the wave! You wonder when it may start to get smaller. While riding this wave, all you can see, hear, touch, smell, and taste is the wave itself. You cannot get your body or mind to feel anything but this giant wave. Your whole body is feeling the pressure and power of the wave. Slowly you notice the wave getting smaller and smaller. The force is turning from giant, to big, to medium, to small, to tiny, to flat. You have a glimpse of the shore ahead of you. You start paddling and find yourself getting closer and closer to the shore. Soon enough, you can plant your feet on the bottom of the ocean floor. You can easily walk to shore. The weight and power of the wave is behind you. You feel lighter and at ease. With your feet back on solid ground, you turn around and watch the power and rhythm of the waves. You notice how giant the waves are when they are far from shore, and how they get smaller and calmer, always coming back to shore.

---

3   This activity is based on an exercise from the wonderful attachment-based treatment model Theraplay (The Theraplay Institute).

When we have a big, powerful feeling it's just like riding a wave. It starts out small, then can grow and grow, until it reaches its highest peak. Just like waves, our feelings always come down from this peak. When the feeling is so big, it takes over our whole body and mind. But feelings always get smaller, all on their own. Feelings are like waves: they come and go. Just remember, even after a big wave, you always come back to shore.

ANOTHER BEDTIME STORY: THE DAY YOU WERE BORN

Most kids love to hear about the day they were born or brought into your family through adoption. Tell your child, in as much detail as you can, about the day they were born. What was the weather like that day? Who was there? How did you feel? If your child was adopted and you don't know all of the details, share what you can. It's okay to say that you wish you knew more!

PART 4
JUST FOR KIDS!

CHAPTER 16

ACTIVITIES JUST FOR KIDS

This chapter is just for kids but feel free to share with your grown-up or ask them if you need help!

I KNOW WHO I AM

Getting to know *you*! The more you know about yourself, the better you can become at working with your emotions.

My favorite color is:

_____

_____

My favorite animal is:

_____

_____

If I could have any superpower, it would be:

_____

_____

My favorite dessert is:

_____

_____

Next Halloween I will dress as:

_____

_____

Things that make me feel grumpy:

Things that make me happy:

I like (write down all the different kinds of things you like):

I dislike (write down all the different kinds of things you don't like):

I get mad when:

_____

_____

_____

_____

I get sad when:

_____

_____

_____

_____

WOULD YOU RATHER?

→ Stare at a blank wall for 15 minutes. **-or-** Wear a wet sock for an hour.

→ Listen to the same song over and over again for two hours. **-or-** Stand in a smelly garbage dump for five minutes.

→ Walk up and down a hallway 100 times. **-or-** Eat a bug.

Which is better for you? Worse?

_____

_____

_____

_____

_____

_____

The **SELF-REGULATION** Workbook for Children Ages 5 to 8

Why?

_____

- -

_____

_____

- -

_____

Clues:

→ If you prefer the staring, listening, or walking options, you may be a kid who deals better with boredom than with things that make you uncomfortable.

→ If you would rather wear a wet sock, stand in the garbage dump, and eat a bug, you may be a kid who is okay with being a little uncomfortable, but cannot stand to be bored!

→ If you were half and half, you may be okay with boredom sometimes and okay with discomfort other times.

BEING A KINDNESS GENIE

Doing something kind for someone we love can give us a good feeling inside. Being a Kindness Genie means doing something nice for someone without them even expecting it! Here are a few fun examples:

→ Draw a picture for someone you love.

→ Ask someone, "How was your day?"

→ Offer someone a bite of what you are having.

→ Write someone a nice note and leave it under their pillow; it can say "I love you!"

→ Give someone a compliment (that means saying something nice to them, like, "I love your smile!").

→ Set the table without your parent asking first.

→ Help clean up the mess someone else may have made (like your sibling).

→ Pick a flower, shell, leaf, or something else from nature for someone.

→ Make a family member's bed for them, or fluff their pillows.

→ Tell someone "I love you," just because.

→ Give your grown-up a hug.

→ Do a chore for your pet without your parent asking first (refill their water, etc.).

→ Tell your parent they did a "great job" on something, like the meal they made.

→ Point out when you see someone being kind to someone else.

→ Help put away groceries.

→ Your own idea:

_____

_____

_____

IF I CAN DO THIS... I CAN DO THAT

We know that kids can do amazing things, including change the world! Kids do many hard things and can use their feelings and experience as superpowers. When you do one hard thing, did you know that it can help you to do more hard things? Here is a list to help you think of all the things you can do:

→ If I can learn to tie my shoes... I can learn how to read.

→ If I can score a goal at a game... I can finish a puzzle.

→ If I can wait 10 minutes for a treat... I can wait my turn for the piñata!

When you do hard things you can do more hard things. See if you can figure out what you *can* do even if you haven't tried it before!

REAL-LIFE EXAMPLE

"My daughter was having a severe case of allergies and needed to take her very first pill to treat them. She was very worried about swallowing a pill and thought she would not be able to do it. I reminded her of an experience to help her: her performance. At this performance, she was so nervous! With support, she was able to gather her courage and performed beautifully. With this recent memory in mind, I said to her, 'If you could do your piano recital, you can swallow this pill.' I could see a shift in her eyes as she started to believe this. With this reminder of this sense of herself, a person who can do hard things even when she is scared, she was able to swallow the pill and feel much better!"

This is the end of the Just for Kids section. Now you can give this back to your grown-up!

FINAL THOUGHTS

Supporting the development of emotion regulation in children ages five through eight is no easy task. It requires our time, attention, and patience. Much of this growth happens naturally. At the same time, there are efforts we can make as caregivers to facilitate its development. As much as we want these skills to take hold, both for our children and for ourselves as caregivers, the stage when our children have unrestrained and intense emotion has its magic and gifts. As parents we get to experience the "profound love" (Gopnik 2016) of accepting, admiring, and delighting in something that is imperfect, that is, our children. What a gift to be in the presence of someone who can feel deeply, express their needs directly, and experience pure, unadulterated joy! We also learn more about our adult selves; in our efforts to support and love our imperfect children, we can appreciate and learn to accept our own imperfections. For adults who did not have loving, supportive caregivers, this stage in a child's life presents a unique opportunity for deep healing; we can do for our children what we did not have ourselves. For our children, this time marks one of the few phases in their lives when being as mad, sad, frustrated or happy as your body and mind wants you to be is natural and easy. It's a time when the body-mind-behavior connection is fluid and free, before we have begun to internalize judgments about our feelings. It's a rare freedom that we can admire and respect about children this age.

Self-regulation is a skill that develops differently for everyone; we hope that this workbook has offered you the reflection, tools and developmental knowledge to set both you and your child on the right foot.

BIBLIOGRAPHY

Allen, Jon, Peter Fonagy, and Anthony Bateman. *Mentalizing in Clinical Practice*. Washington, DC: American Psychiatric Press, 2008.

Bandura, Albert. "Self-Efficacy: Toward a Unifying Theory of Behavioral Change." *Psychological Review*. 84, no. 2 (1977): 191–215.

Barish, Kenneth. *Pride & Joy: A Guide to Understanding Your Child's Emotions and Solving Family Problems*. New York: Oxford University Press, 2012.

Beebe, Beatrice, and Miriam Steele. "How Does Microanalysis of Mother–Infant Communication Inform Maternal Sensitivity and Infant Attachment?" *Attachment & Human Development 15*, no. 5–6 (2013): 583–602.

Bowlby, John. *Attachment and Loss, Volume 2: Separation: Anxiety and Anger*. London: Hogarth Press and Institute of Psycho-Analysis, 1973.

Cline, Foster, and Jim Fay. *Parenting with Love and Logic: Teaching Children Responsibility, Third Edition*. Colorado Springs, CO: NavPress, 2020.

Dennison, Paul E., and Gail E. Dennison. *Brain Gym, Teachers Edition*. Ventura, California: Edu-Kinesthetics, 1994.

Doucleff, Michaeleen, and Jane Greenhalgh. "How Inuit Parents Teach Kids to Control Their Anger." *NPR's Science Desk: The Other Side of Anger*, March 13, 2019.

Erikson, Erik. *Identity: Youth and Crisis*. New York: Norton, 1968.

Felitti, Vincent J., Robert F. Anda, Dale Nordenberg, et al. "Relationship of Childhood Abuse and Household Dysfunction to Many of the Leading Causes of Death in Adults: The Adverse Childhood Experiences (ACE) Study." *American Journal of Preventive Medicine* 14, no. 4 (1998): 245–258.

Fonagy, P., G. Gergely, E. Jurist, et al. *Affect Regulation, Mentalization, and the Development of the Self*. New York: Other Press, 2002.

Fosha, Diana, ed. *Undoing Aloneness and the Transformation of Suffering into Flourishing: AEDP 2.0*. Washington, DC: American Psychological Association, 2021.

Fosha, Diana. "Emotion: The Vitality Affects." Presentation, April 2013.

Gopnik, Alison. *The Gardener and the Carpenter: What the New Science of Child Development Tells Us about the Relationship between Parents and Children*. New York: Picador, 2016.

Greene, Ross W. *The Explosive Child* [Sixth Edition]. New York, New York: HarperCollins, 2021.

Hawkes, Kristen, and James E. Coxworth. "Grandmothers and the Evolution of Human Longevity: A Review of Findings and Future Directions." *Evolutionary Anthropology: Issues, News, and Reviews 22*, no. 6 (2013): 294–302. Accessed July 1, 2024.

Holbrook, Jessica. "Building Adaptive Skills in Children with Disabilities." WonderBaby.org. June 18, 2023. https://www.wonderbaby.org/articles/adaptive-skills.

Hughes, Daniel. *Attachment-Focused Parenting: Effective Strategies to Care for Children.* New York: W. W. Norton & Company, Inc., 2009.

Linehan, M. *Cognitive-Behavioral Treatment of Borderline Personality Disorder*. New York: Guilford Publications, 1993.

Ludy-Dobson, Christine, and Bruce Perry. "The Role of Healthy Relational Interactions in Buffering the Impact of Childhood Trauma." In Gil, Eliana (ed.) *Working with Children to Heal Interpersonal Trauma: The Power of Play.* New York: The Guilford Press, 2010.

Midgley, Nick, and Ioanna Vrouva, eds. *Minding the Child: Mentalization-Based Interventions with Children, Young People, and Their Families.* East Sussex, Routledge, UK: 2012.

Mischel, Walter, Ebbe B. Ebbesen, and Antonette Raskoff Zeiss. "Cognitive and Attentional Mechanisms in Delay of Gratification." *Journal of Personality and Social Psychology* 21, no. 2 (1972): 204–218.

National Alliance on Mental Illness. "Validating & Invalidating Statements and Curious Questions." https://namibrevard.org/Information/Validating-and-Invalidating-Statements.pdf.

National Scientific Council on the Developing Child. 2015. *Supportive Relationships and Active Skill-Building Strengthen the Foundations of Resilience: Working Paper 13.* http://www.developingchild.harvard.edu.

Novick, Kerry K., and Jack Novick. *Emotional Muscle: Strong Parents, Strong Children.* Bloomington, IN: Xlibris, 2010.

Purvis, Karyn B., David R. Cross, and Wendy L. Sunshine. *The Connected Child: Bring Hope and Healing to Your Adoptive Family.* New York: McGraw Hill, 2007.

Siegel, Daniel, and Mary Hartzell. *Parenting from the Inside Out: How a Deeper Self-Understanding Can Help You Raise Children Who Thrive.* New York: Jeremy P. Tarcher/Penguin, 2013.

Siegel, Daniel, and Tina P. Bryson. *The Whole-Brain Child: 12 Revolutionary Strategies to Nurture Your Child's Developing Mind, Survive Everyday Parenting Struggles, and Help Your Family Thrive.* New York: Bantam Books, 2012

Slade, Arietta. "Parental Reflective Functioning: An Introduction." *Attachment & Human Development 7*, no. 3 (2005): 269–281.

Slade, Arietta with Lois S. Sadler, Tanika Eaves, and Denise L. Webb. *Enhancing Attachment and Reflective Parenting in Clinical Practice: A Minding the Baby Approach.* New York: Guilford Publications, 2023.

Sorenson, Pamela. "Changing Positions: Helping Parents Look through the Child's Eyes." *Journal of Child Psychotherapy 31*, no. 2 (2005): 153–168.

Stixrud, William, and Ned Johnson. *The Self-Driven Child*. New York: Penguin Books, 2018.

Straus, Martha. *Cool, Calm, and Connected: A Workbook for Parents and Children to Co-Regulate, Manage Big Emotions, and Build Stronger Bonds*. Eau Claire, WI: PESI Publishing, 2021.

Tottenham, Nim. "Development of Emotion Regulation Neurobiology and the Role of the Parent." Conference Presentation, NeuroSchool, February 17, 2023.

Tronick, Edward. "Emotions and Emotional Communication in Infants." *American Psychologist 44*, no. 2 (1989): 112–119.

Tyson, Phyllis. and Robert Tyson, *Psychoanalytic Theories of Development: An Integration*. New Haven, CT: Yale University, 1990.

Voss, Angie. *Understanding Your Child's Sensory Signals*. Angie Voss, 2011.

Winnicott, Donald. *Playing and Reality*. New York: Routledge Classics, 1971.

Wipfler, Patty, and Tosha Schore. *Listen: Five Simple Tools to Meet Your Everyday Parenting Challenges*. Palo Alto, CA: Hand in Hand Parenting, 2016.

ACKNOWLEDGMENTS

From Kahlila: This workbook is the culmination of decades of personal and professional hard work, and I am so grateful to the many people who have offered their love and guidance to me along the way. First and foremost, I would like to thank my husband for his steadfast support, devoted friendship, and wise counsel. Thank you for being my secure base, helping me to be brave, and always making me laugh. Thank you to my children for being my greatest teachers and the reason this workbook exists! Thank you, Sasie, for the humor and sparkle you bring to every day, and for the excellent edits and feedback you provided on this workbook. Austin, thank you so much for your incredibly sweet and positive energy, and for your boosts of love and encouragement.

I would like to thank my father, who sang to me often and was very attuned to me at a young age, and my mother, who has offered me unconditional love and is still naughtily playful. Thank you also to my sister, who championed this project from the start. I would like to thank many colleagues, including Alea Holman, PhD, and Leah Crane, PhD, both early readers and supporters of this project. I have been lucky enough to have numerous superb mentors, including those who introduced me to many of the concepts and approaches discussed in this workbook, and who have deeply supported my professional development: Arietta Slade, PhD, Ken Barish, PhD, Miguelina German, PhD, and Courtney Rennicke, PhD.

I would very much like to thank other generous colleagues who offered their time and care to me in the production of this book: Carolyn Sorkin, PhD, and Nanika Coor, PsyD. I also have to thank a number of dear friends who helped bring this workbook to life. Thank you to the hundreds of parents and children I have worked with, who have offered their vulnerability, hearts, and minds, and taught me so much of what I know about parent and child self-regulation. Finally, I'd like to thank Sarah Gerstenzang, who could not have been a better complement to me in this process.

This workbook is dedicated to Rachel Brown and Roxsian Sharpe, two talented, whole-hearted, burgeoning therapists who would surely have contributed to our field.

From Sarah: This workbook reflects so much of our own experience being parented as well as parenting ourselves and for that I want to acknowledge my own mother who always made me feel safe and cared for—one of my earliest memories was of not wanting to leave her side. And her mother, my grandmother, who made me feel loved.

I want to acknowledge my children, Sam, Emma, and Lily who have brought me joy that made my whole life feel meaningful every single day; and my husband, Michael, who not only was a fabulous and fun parenting partner but also helped me see through his fathering what I missed with my own. And I also want to thank some of the women who supported me as a parent—my sister, Stephanie Sheffield, PhD, MD, who is both a parenting support to me and a very helpful professional colleague at times. As well as my friend, Lisa Classen Coen, PhD, who is always there to provide insightful personal, parenting and professional advice.

It also reflects our professional experience and in that regard, I want to thank Arleta James, LPCC, who has always made time to mentor me. And thank you to the many parents I have worked with who desperately want close relationships with their children and stretch themselves in ways that I both admire and wish that I could go back in time and emulate in my own not so perfect parenting moments.

Lastly, I want to acknowledge my thoughtful colleague, Kahlila Robinson: thank you for inviting me to collaborate with you. And our editor, Claire Sielaff: a model in communication, which in the end is what this workbook is all about.

ABOUT THE AUTHORS

Kahlila Robinson, PhD, is a psychologist in private practice in New York City. She received her doctoral training from the Graduate Center, City University of New York. She has specialized training and experience working with children and families, in parent mental health, and with adults with relational trauma. She has worked in hospital and clinic settings, as a mental health consultant in preschools, and as director of parent mental health of a nationally recognized early intervention program in the Bronx, New York. She is a supervising psychologist for child and adult psychology graduate students at City College. She is an advocate for the availabilty of high-quality mental health services for underserved and vulnerable populations. She lives with her husband and children in New York City.

Sarah Gerstenzang, LCSW, is passionate about healthy human development. She currently works as a therapist with foster and adoptive families and previously held policy and administrative positions in child welfare. She holds a master's degree in social work from Columbia University. She is the board president of the Adoptive and Foster Family Coalition of NY and has served on numerous advisory committees, including *Fostering Families Today* magazine, the Effects of Early Life Adversity on Brain Development (NIMH grant with Nim Tottenham, PhD), and on the National Adoption Competency Mental Health Training Initiative. Sarah has been a foster and kinship parent and one of her three children was adopted from the New York City foster care system.